GRAPHIC SCIENCE AND ENGINEERING IN ACTION

ENGINEERING A TOTALLY RAD

SKATEBOARD

WITH **MAX AXIOM**
SUPER SCIENTIST

by Tammy Enz

illustrated by Pop Art Studios

Consultant:
Morgan Hynes, PhD
Research Assistant Professor, Education
Research Program Manager
Center for Engineering Education and Outreach
Tufts University
Medford, Massachusetts

CAPSTONE PRESS
a capstone imprint

Graphic Library is published by Capstone Press,
1710 Roe Crest Drive, North Mankato, Minnesota 56003
www.capstonepub.com

Library of Congress Cataloging-in-Publication Data
Enz, Tammy.
  Engineering a totally rad skateboard with Max Axiom, super scientist / by Tammy Enz ;
illustrated by Pop Art Studios.
       pages cm.—(Graphic library. Graphic science and engineering in action)
  Includes bibliographical references and index.
  ISBN 978-1-4296-9935-8 (library binding)
  ISBN 978-1-62065-703-4 (paperback)
  ISBN 978-1-4765-1589-2 (ebook PDF)
  1. Skateboards—Design and construction—Comic books, strips, etc.—Juvenile literature. 2.
Graphic novels. I. Pop Art Studios, illustrator. II. Title.
  TT174.5.S35E59 2013
  741.5—dc23   2012026437

Summary: In graphic novel format, follows Max Axiom as he uses the engineering process to
design and build a skateboard.

Designer
Ted Williams

Production Specialist
Laura Manthe

Cover Illustrator
Marcelo Baez

Editor
Christopher L. Harbo

Media Researcher
Wanda Winch

Printed in the United States of America in Brainerd, Minnesota.
092012   006938BANGS13

TABLE of CONTENTS

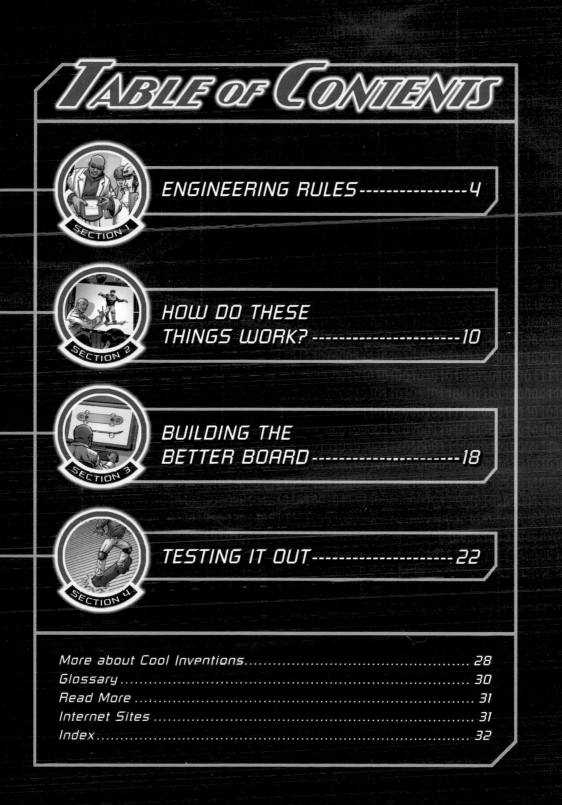

SECTION 1 ENGINEERING RULES

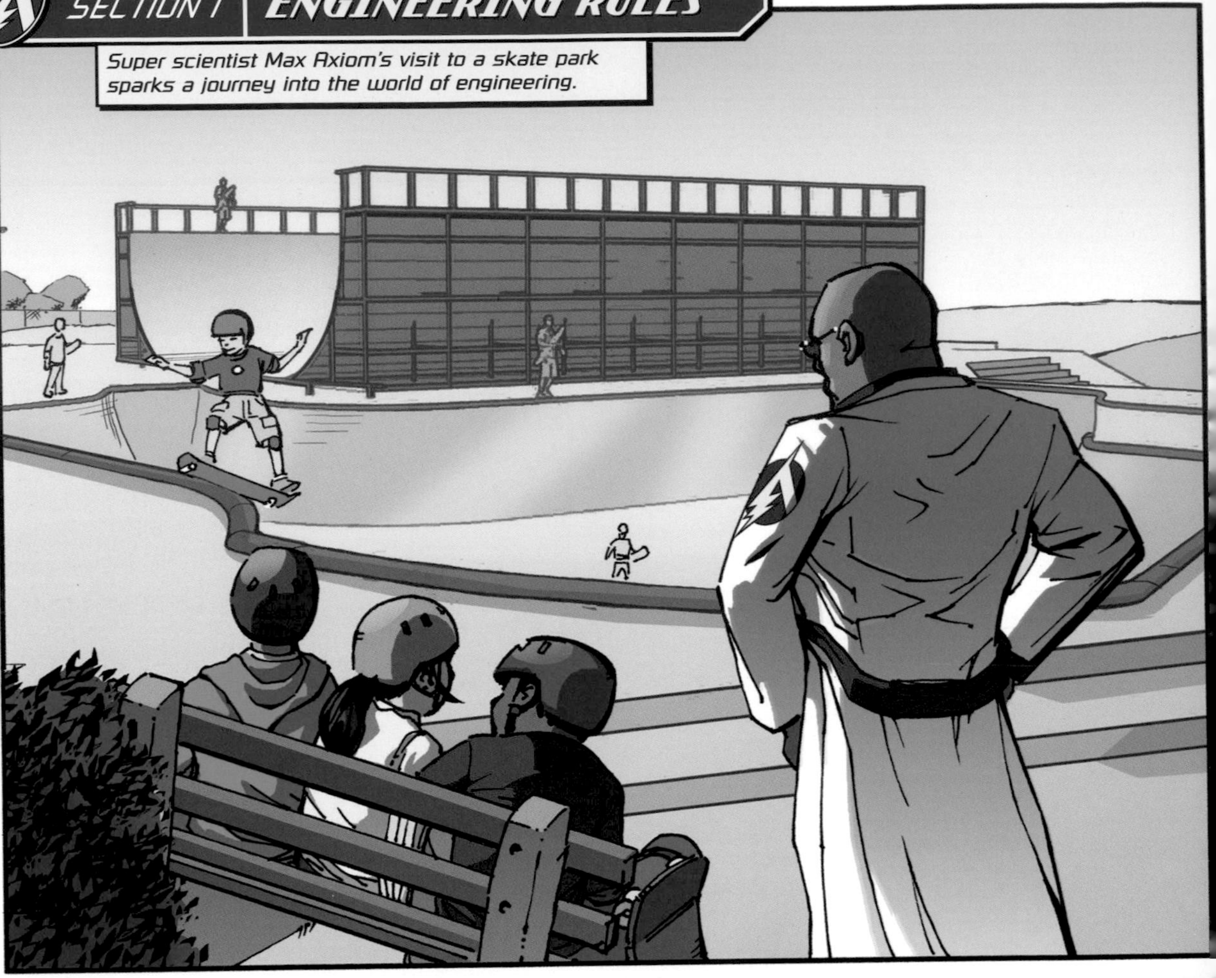
Super scientist Max Axiom's visit to a skate park sparks a journey into the world of engineering.

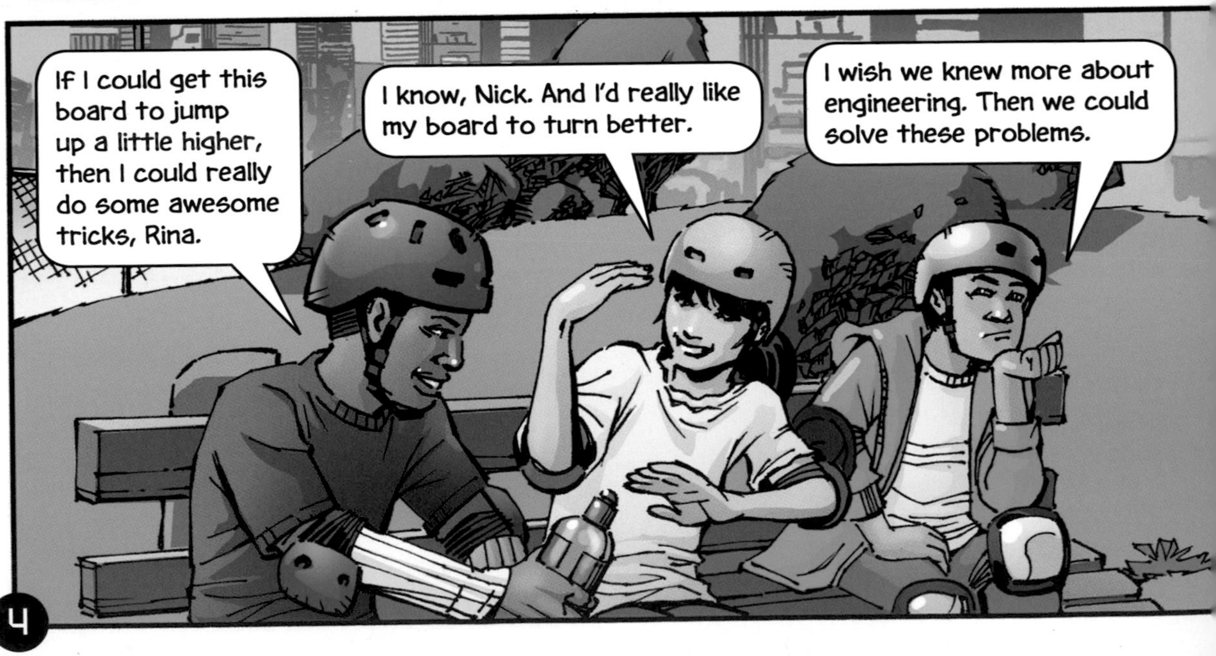
If I could get this board to jump up a little higher, then I could really do some awesome tricks, Rina.
I know, Nick. And I'd really like my board to turn better.
I wish we knew more about engineering. Then we could solve these problems.

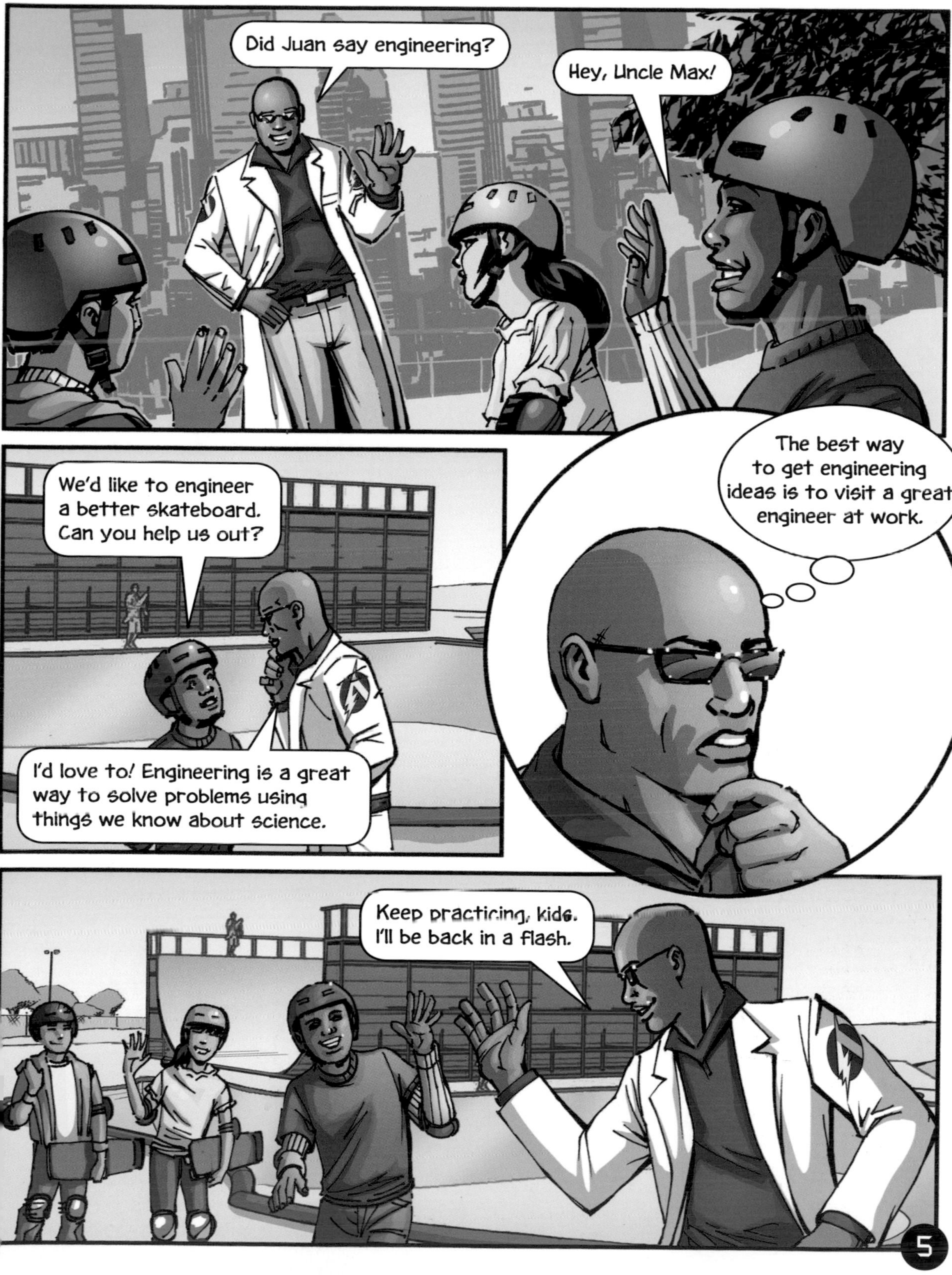
Did Juan say engineering?
Hey, Uncle Max!
We'd like to engineer a better skateboard. Can you help us out?
I'd love to! Engineering is a great way to solve problems using things we know about science.
The best way to get engineering ideas is to visit a great engineer at work.
Keep practicing, kids. I'll be back in a flash.

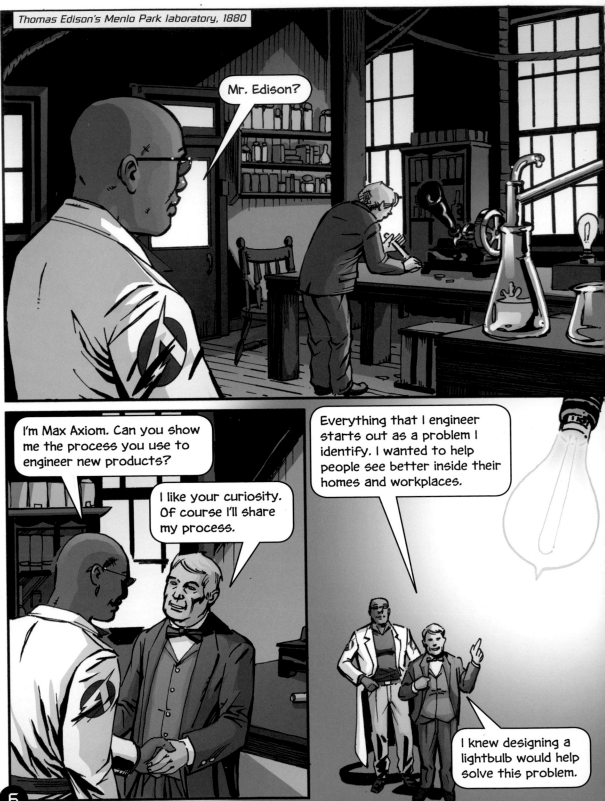

Thomas Edison's Menlo Park laboratory, 1880

Mr. Edison?

I'm Max Axiom. Can you show me the process you use to engineer new products?

I like your curiosity. Of course I'll share my process.

Everything that I engineer starts out as a problem I identify. I wanted to help people see better inside their homes and workplaces.

I knew designing a lightbulb would help solve this problem.

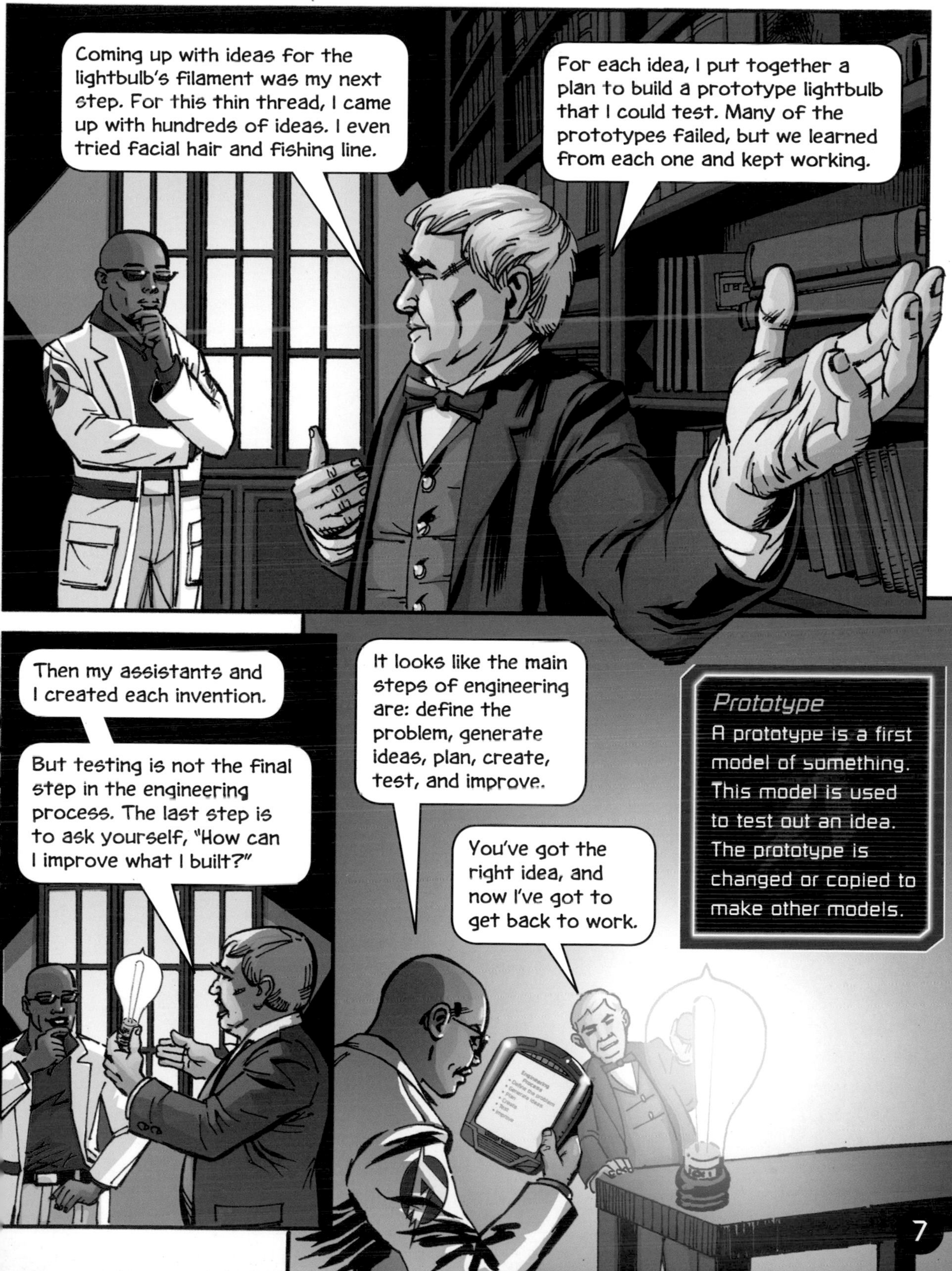
Coming up with ideas for the lightbulb's filament was my next step. For this thin thread, I came up with hundreds of ideas. I even tried facial hair and fishing line.
For each idea, I put together a plan to build a prototype lightbulb that I could test. Many of the prototypes failed, but we learned from each one and kept working.
Then my assistants and I created each invention.
But testing is not the final step in the engineering process. The last step is to ask yourself, "How can I improve what I built?"
It looks like the main steps of engineering are: define the problem, generate ideas, plan, create, test, and improve.
You've got the right idea, and now I've got to get back to work.
Prototype
A prototype is a first model of something. This model is used to test out an idea. The prototype is changed or copied to make other models.

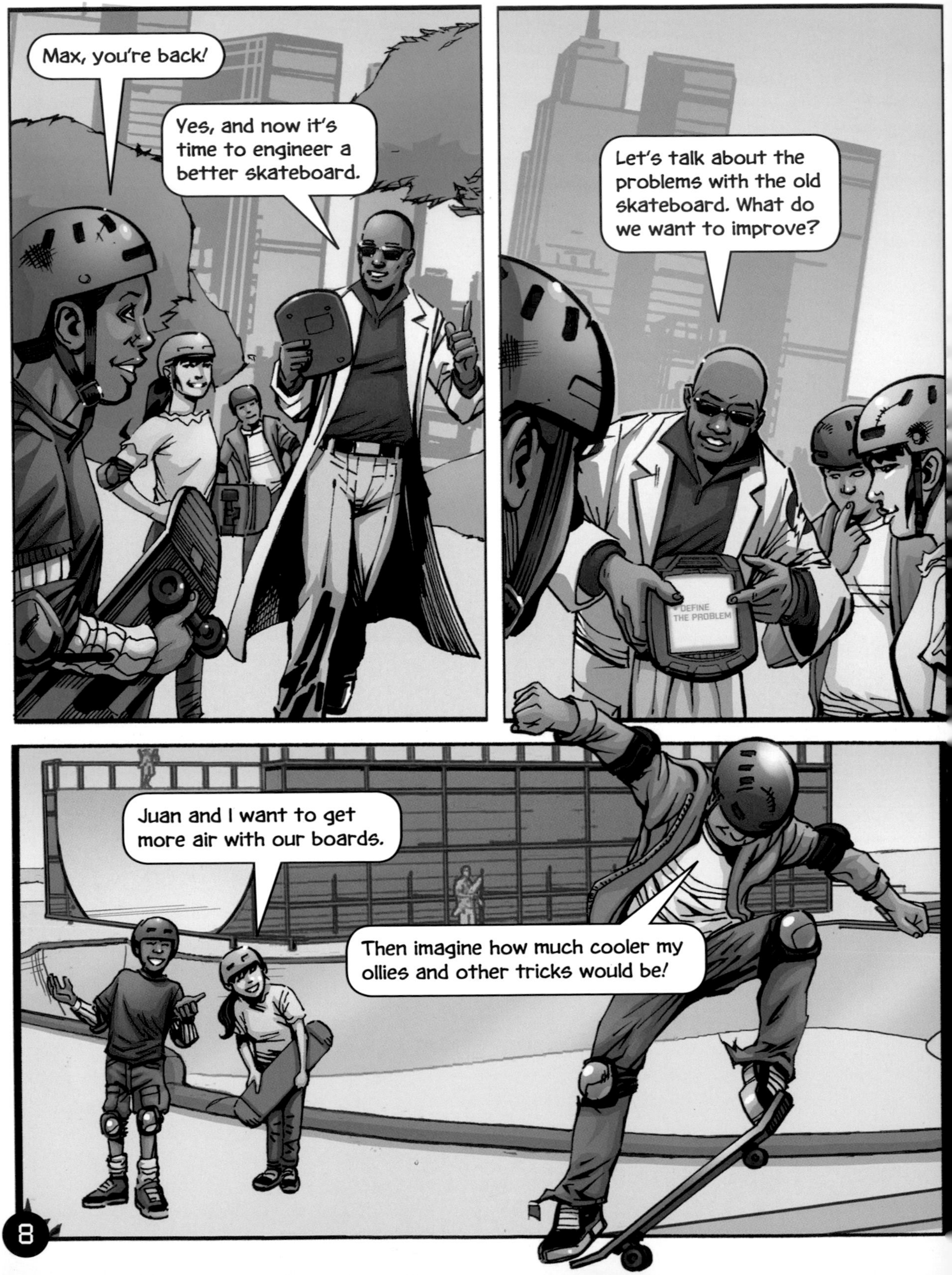
Max, you're back!
Yes, and now it's time to engineer a better skateboard.
Let's talk about the problems with the old skateboard. What do we want to improve?
DEFINE THE PROBLEM
Juan and I want to get more air with our boards.
Then imagine how much cooler my ollies and other tricks would be!

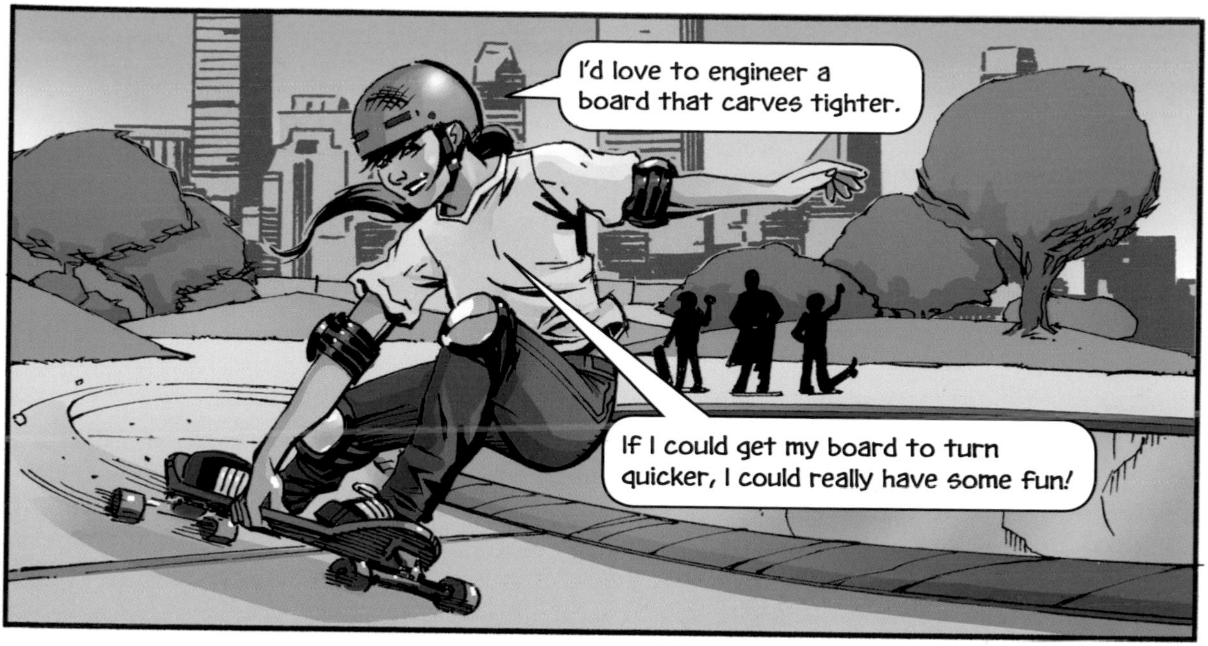
I'd love to engineer a board that carves tighter.
If I could get my board to turn quicker, I could really have some fun!

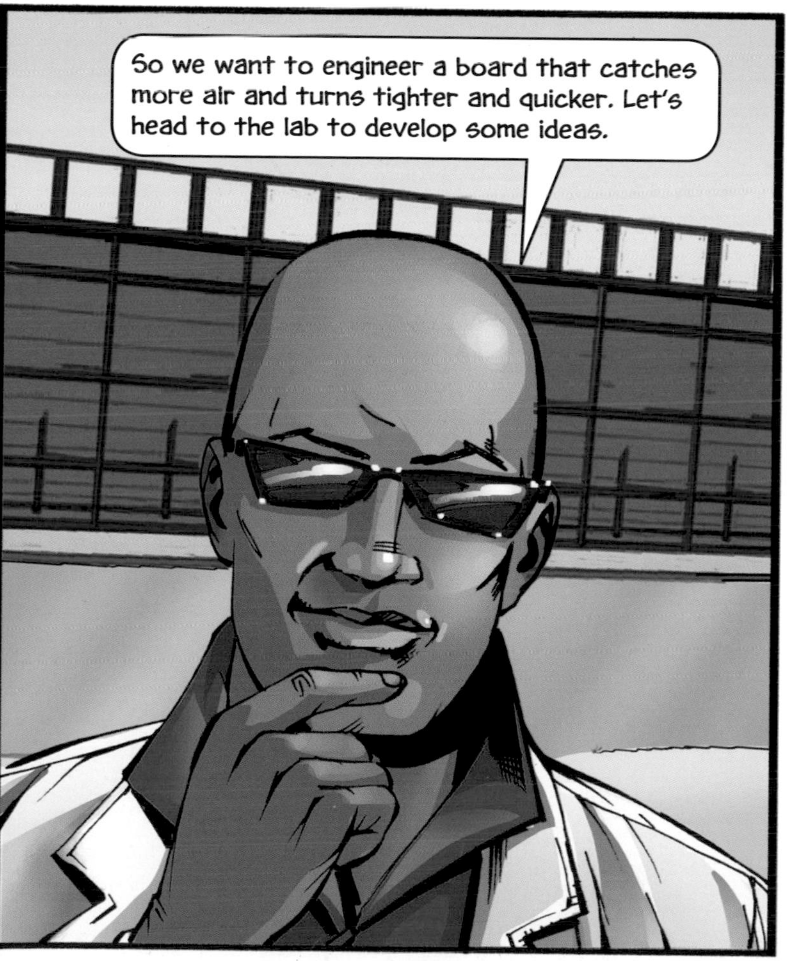
So we want to engineer a board that catches more air and turns tighter and quicker. Let's head to the lab to develop some ideas.

Ollie

The ollie is the basic move in most skating tricks. It is a jumping skill that allows a skater to hop over curbs and obstacles. Skaters jump several feet in the air while the board appears to stick to their feet. Alan Gelfand invented the ollie by accident in 1978. His friends named the move after his nickname—"Ollie."

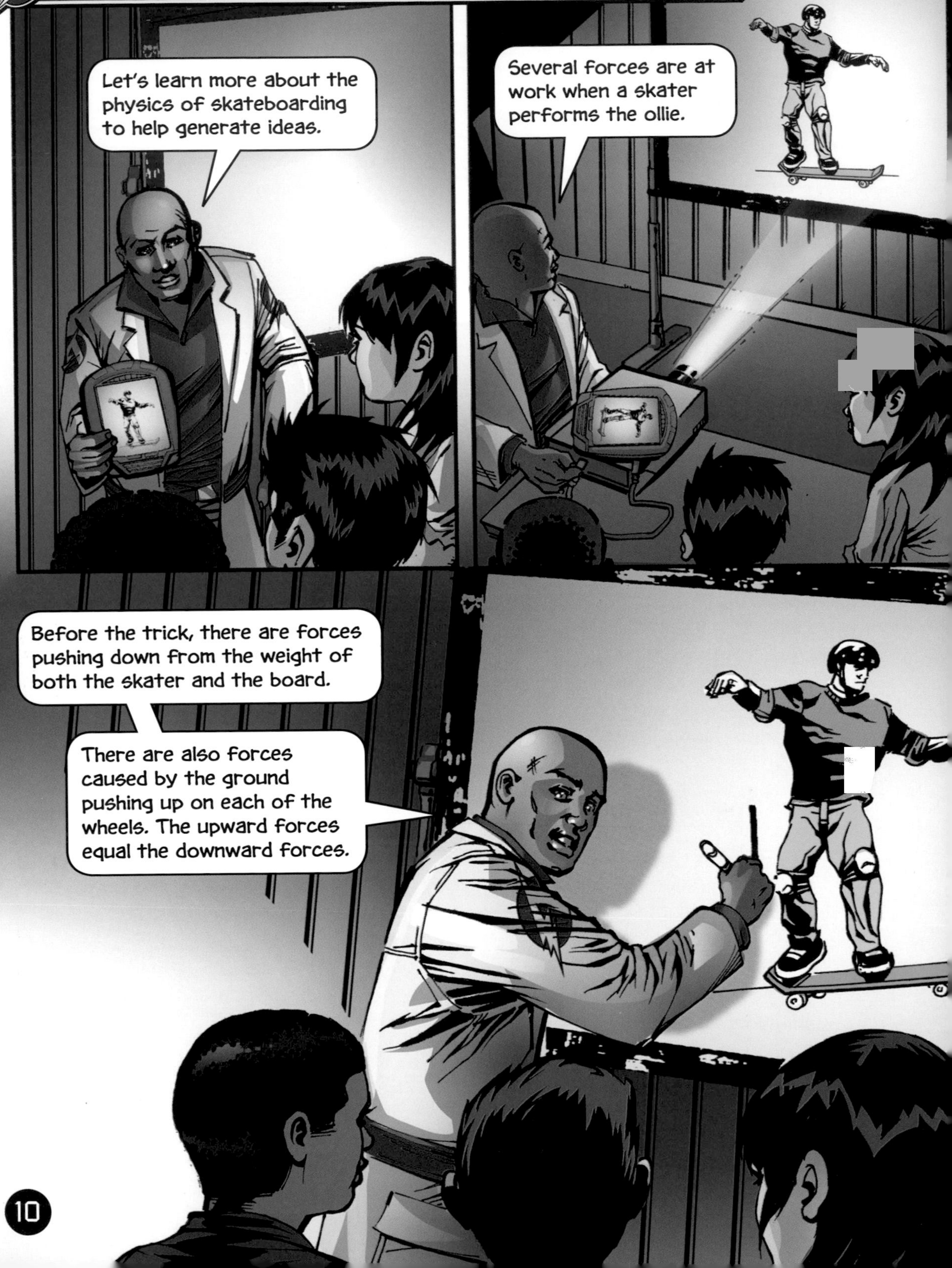
Let's learn more about the physics of skateboarding to help generate ideas.
Several forces are at work when a skater performs the ollie.
Before the trick, there are forces pushing down from the weight of both the skater and the board.
There are also forces caused by the ground pushing up on each of the wheels. The upward forces equal the downward forces.

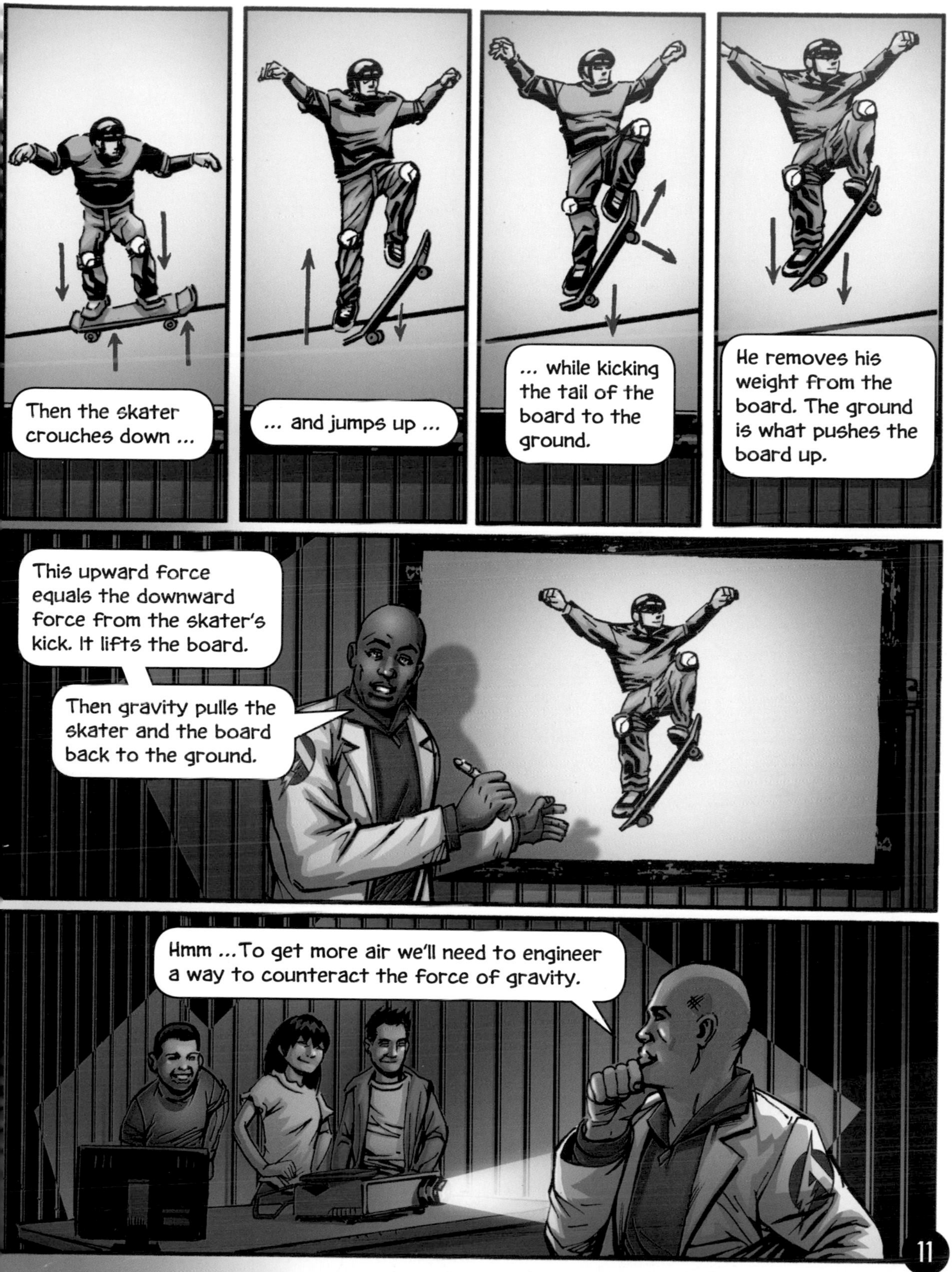
Then the skater crouches down ...
... and jumps up ...
... while kicking the tail of the board to the ground.
He removes his weight from the board. The ground is what pushes the board up.
This upward force equals the downward force from the skater's kick. It lifts the board.
Then gravity pulls the skater and the board back to the ground.
Hmm ...To get more air we'll need to engineer a way to counteract the force of gravity.

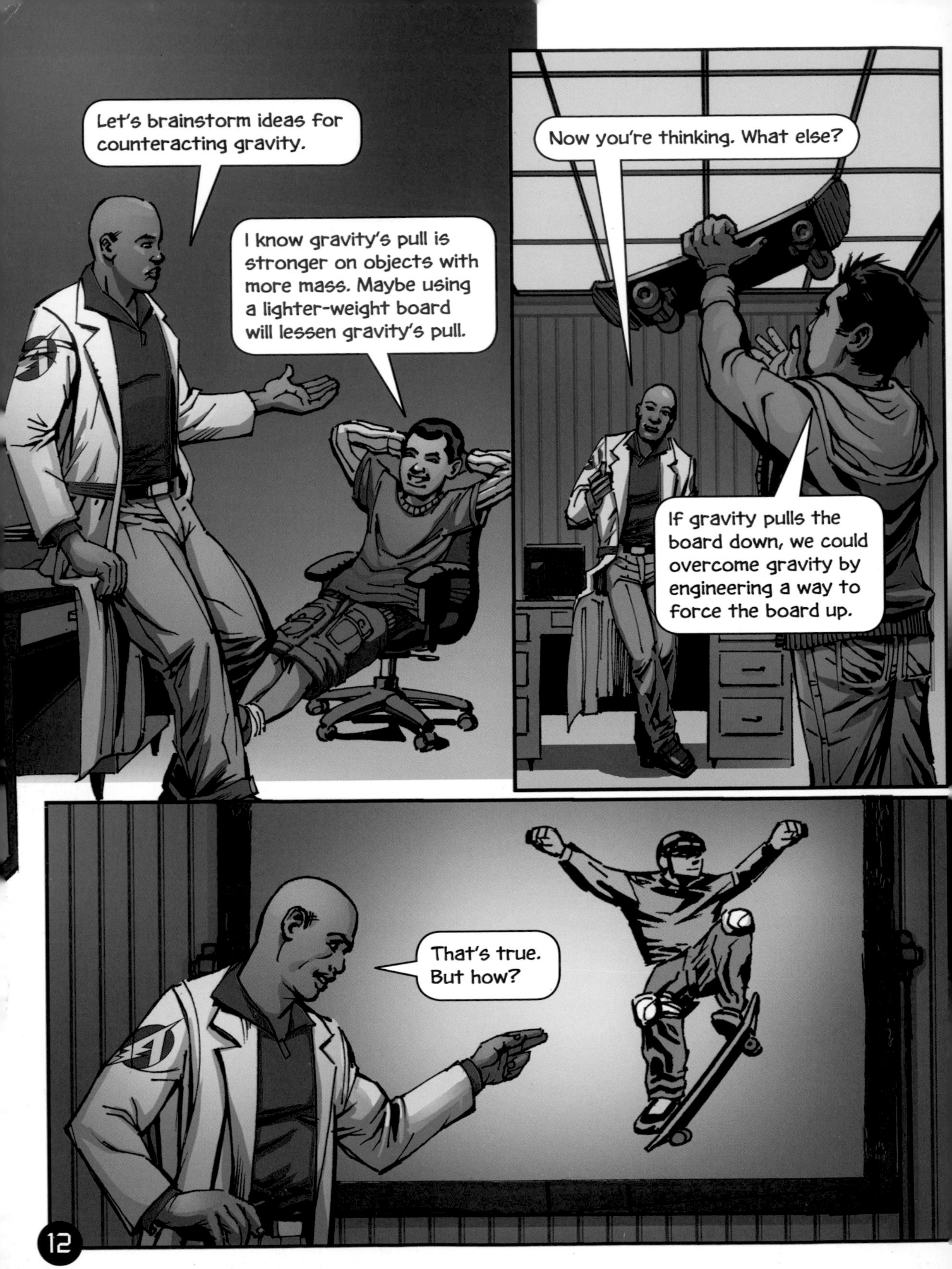
Let's brainstorm ideas for counteracting gravity.
I know gravity's pull is stronger on objects with more mass. Maybe using a lighter-weight board will lessen gravity's pull.
Now you're thinking. What else?
If gravity pulls the board down, we could overcome gravity by engineering a way to force the board up.
That's true. But how?

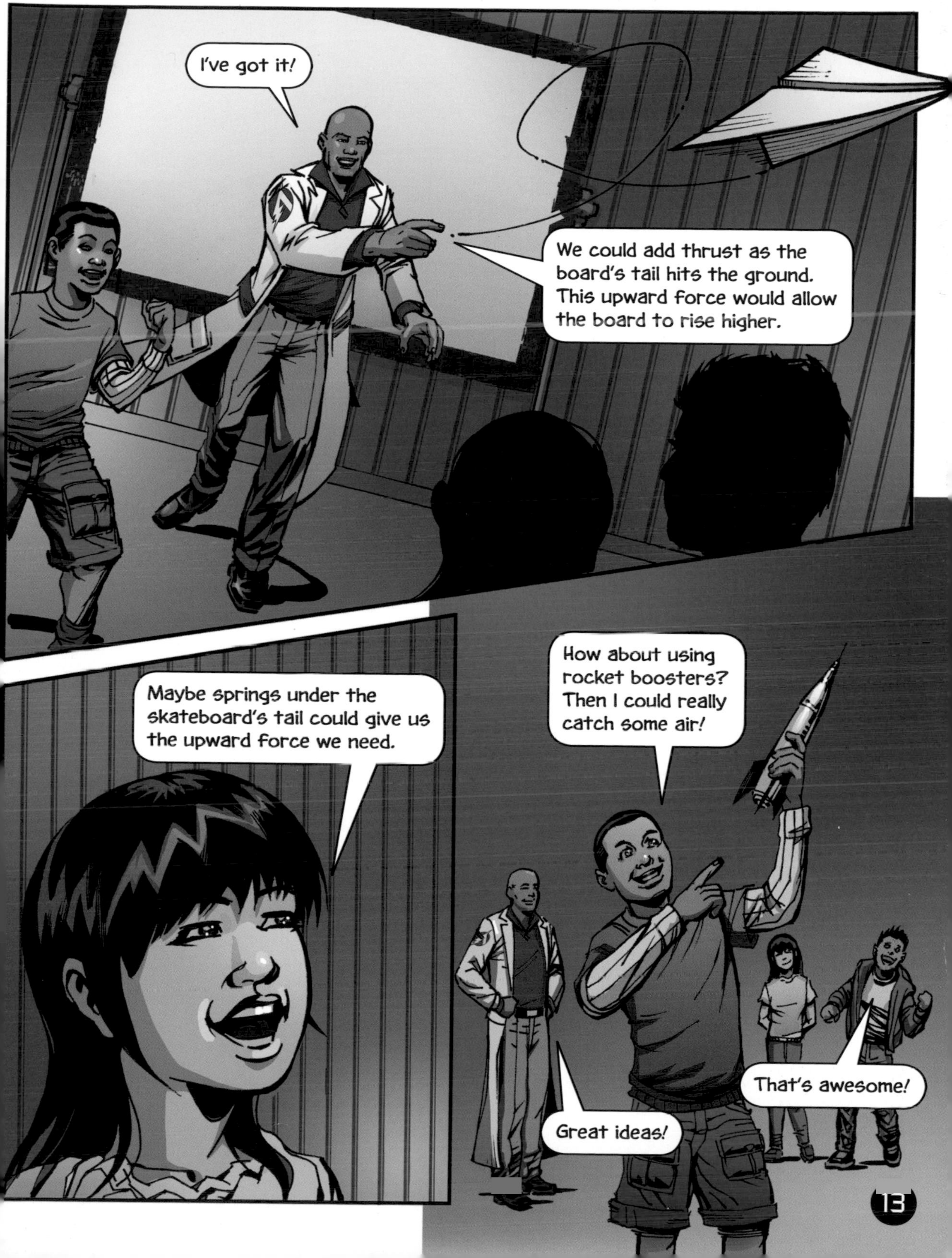
I've got it!
We could add thrust as the board's tail hits the ground. This upward force would allow the board to rise higher.
Maybe springs under the skateboard's tail could give us the upward force we need.
How about using rocket boosters? Then I could really catch some air!
That's awesome!
Great ideas!

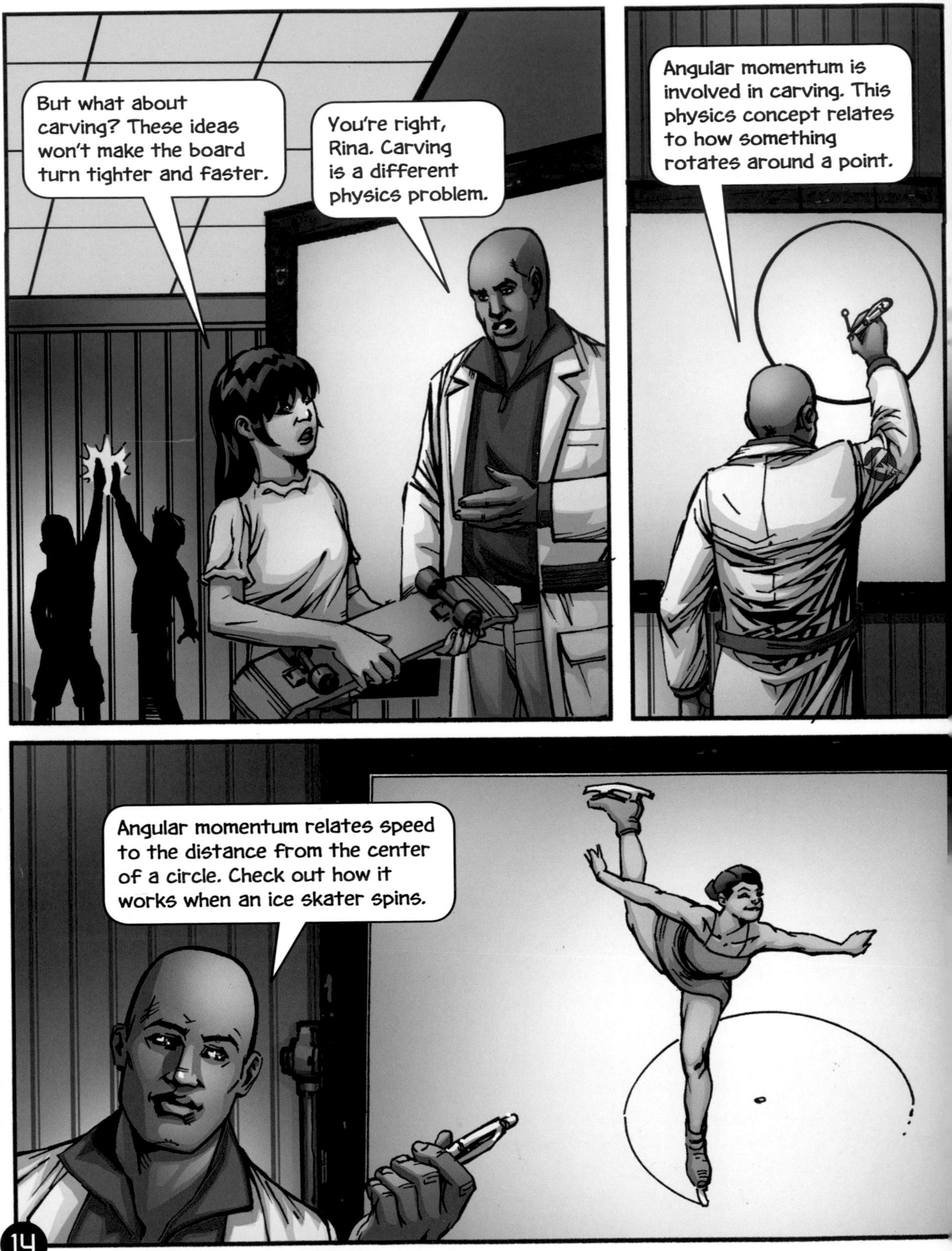
But what about carving? These ideas won't make the board turn tighter and faster.
You're right, Rina. Carving is a different physics problem.
Angular momentum is involved in carving. This physics concept relates to how something rotates around a point.
Angular momentum relates speed to the distance from the center of a circle. Check out how it works when an ice skater spins.

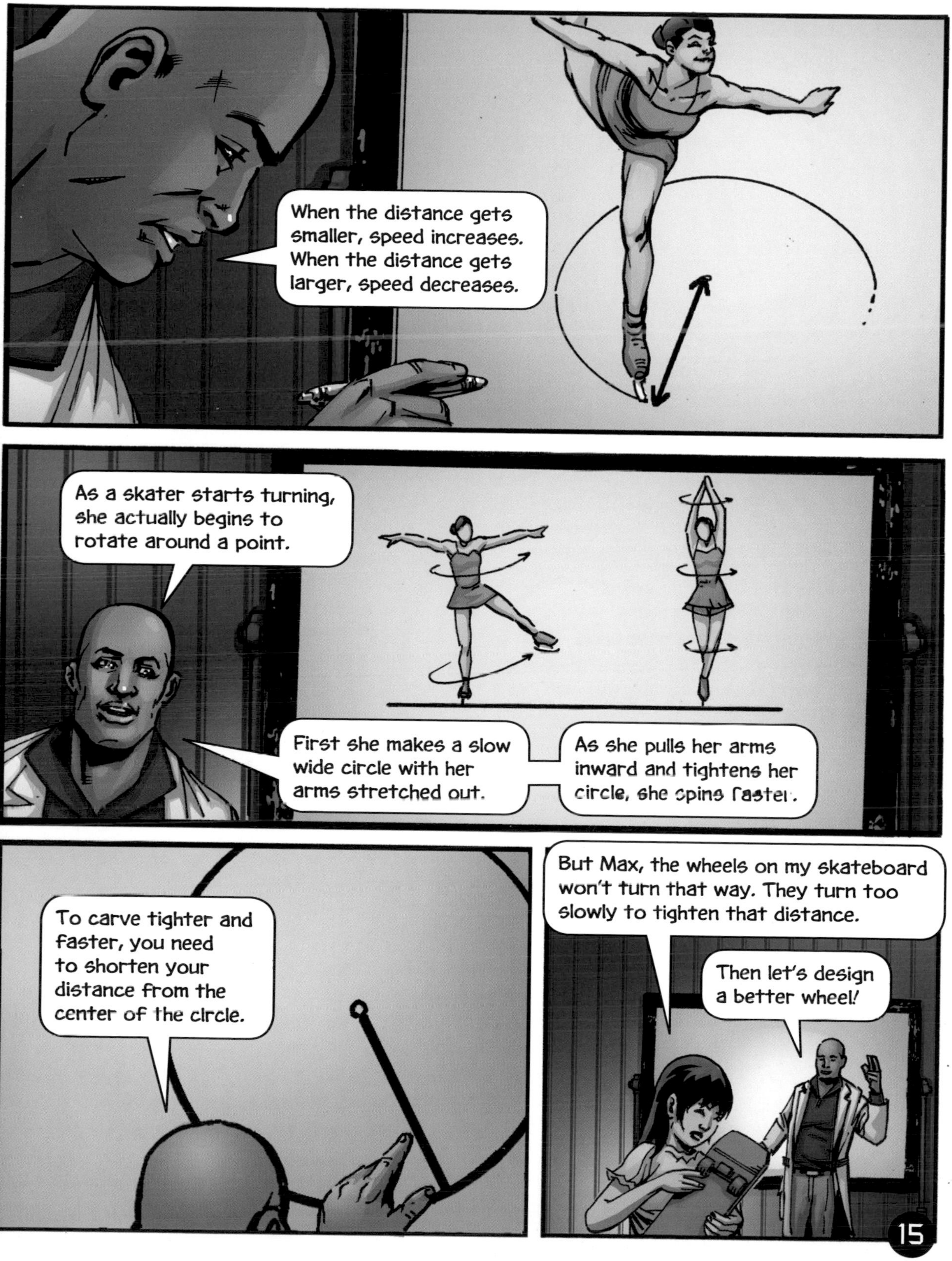
When the distance gets smaller, speed increases. When the distance gets larger, speed decreases.
As a skater starts turning, she actually begins to rotate around a point.
First she makes a slow wide circle with her arms stretched out.
As she pulls her arms inward and tightens her circle, she spins faster.
To carve tighter and faster, you need to shorten your distance from the center of the circle.
But Max, the wheels on my skateboard won't turn that way. They turn too slowly to tighten that distance.
Then let's design a better wheel!

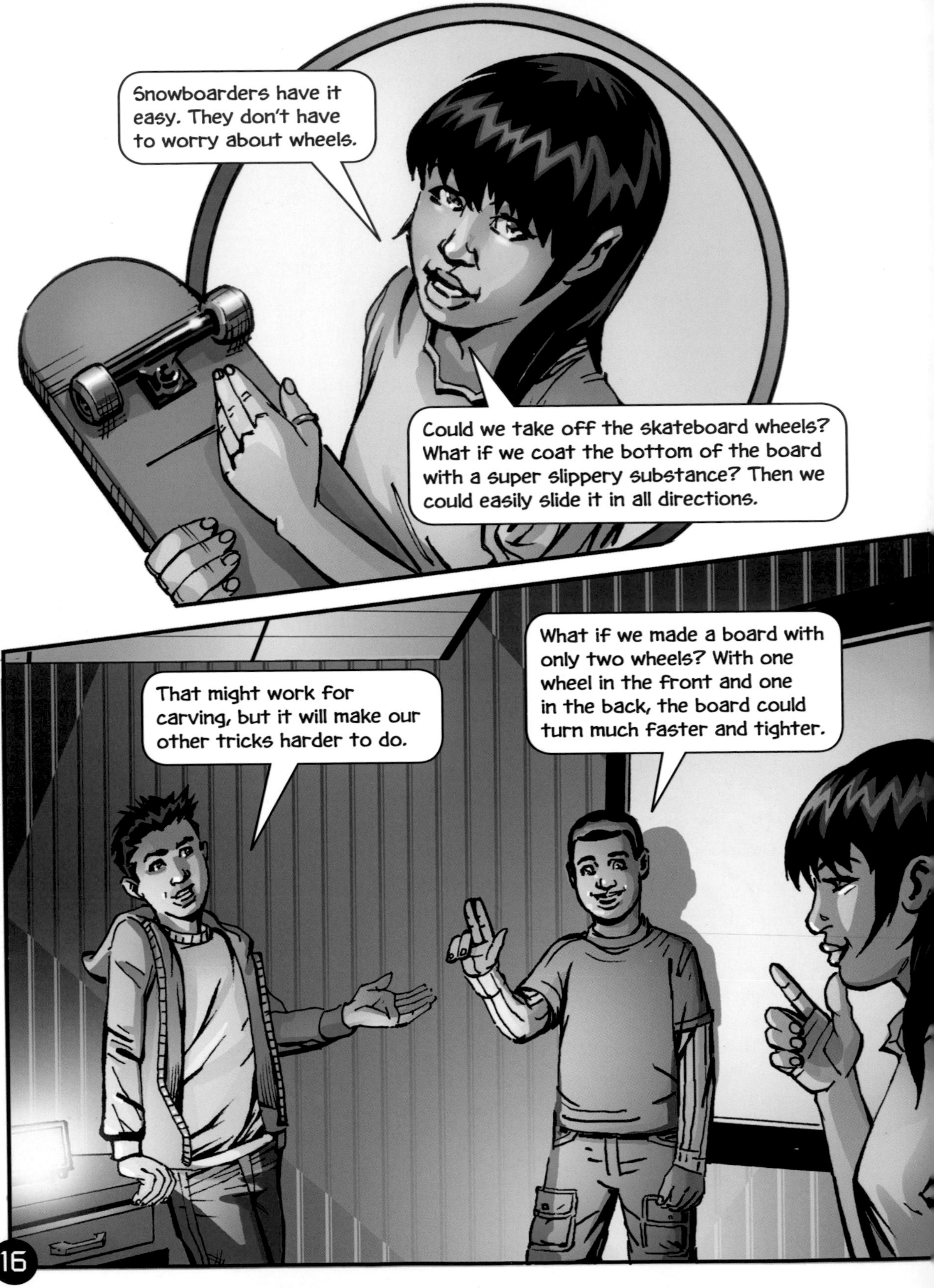
Snowboarders have it easy. They don't have to worry about wheels.
Could we take off the skateboard wheels? What if we coat the bottom of the board with a super slippery substance? Then we could easily slide it in all directions.
That might work for carving, but it will make our other tricks harder to do.
What if we made a board with only two wheels? With one wheel in the front and one in the back, the board could turn much faster and tighter.

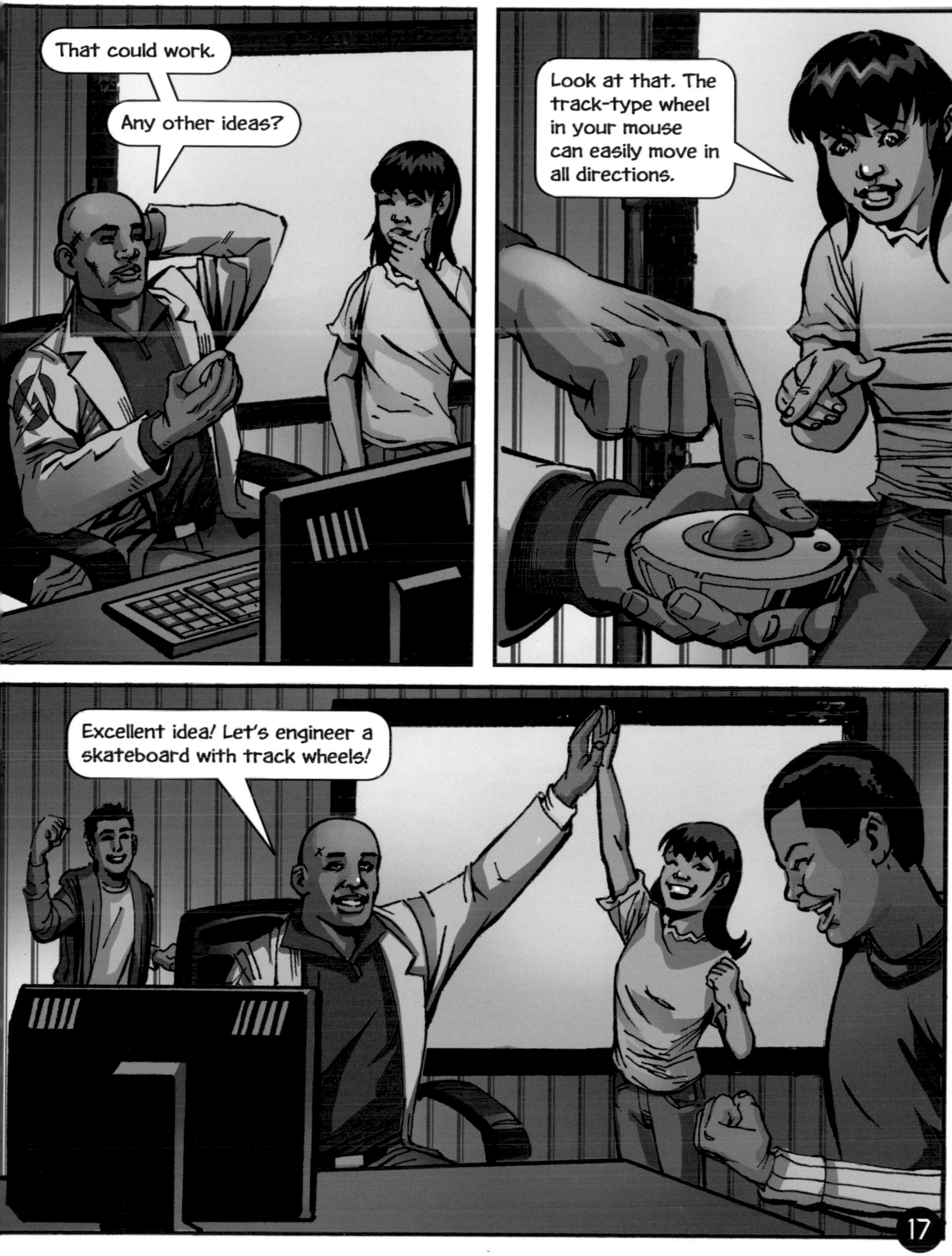
That could work.
Any other ideas?
Look at that. The track-type wheel in your mouse can easily move in all directions.
Excellent idea! Let's engineer a skateboard with track wheels!

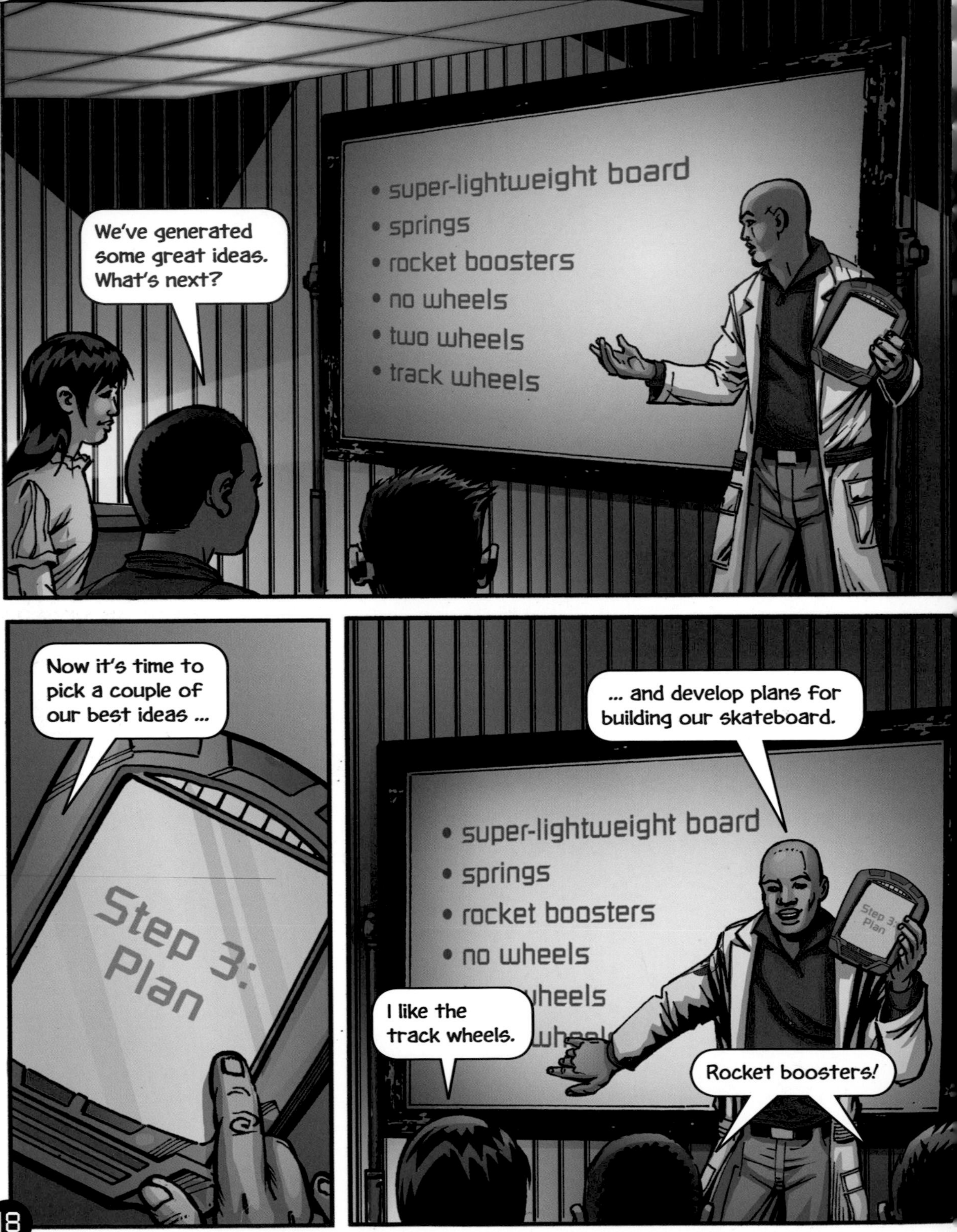
• super-lightweight board
• springs
• rocket boosters
• no wheels
• two wheels
• track wheels
We've generated some great ideas. What's next?
Now it's time to pick a couple of our best ideas ...
Step 3: Plan
... and develop plans for building our skateboard.
• super-lightweight board
• springs
• rocket boosters
• no wheels
Step 3: Plan
I like the track wheels.
Rocket boosters!

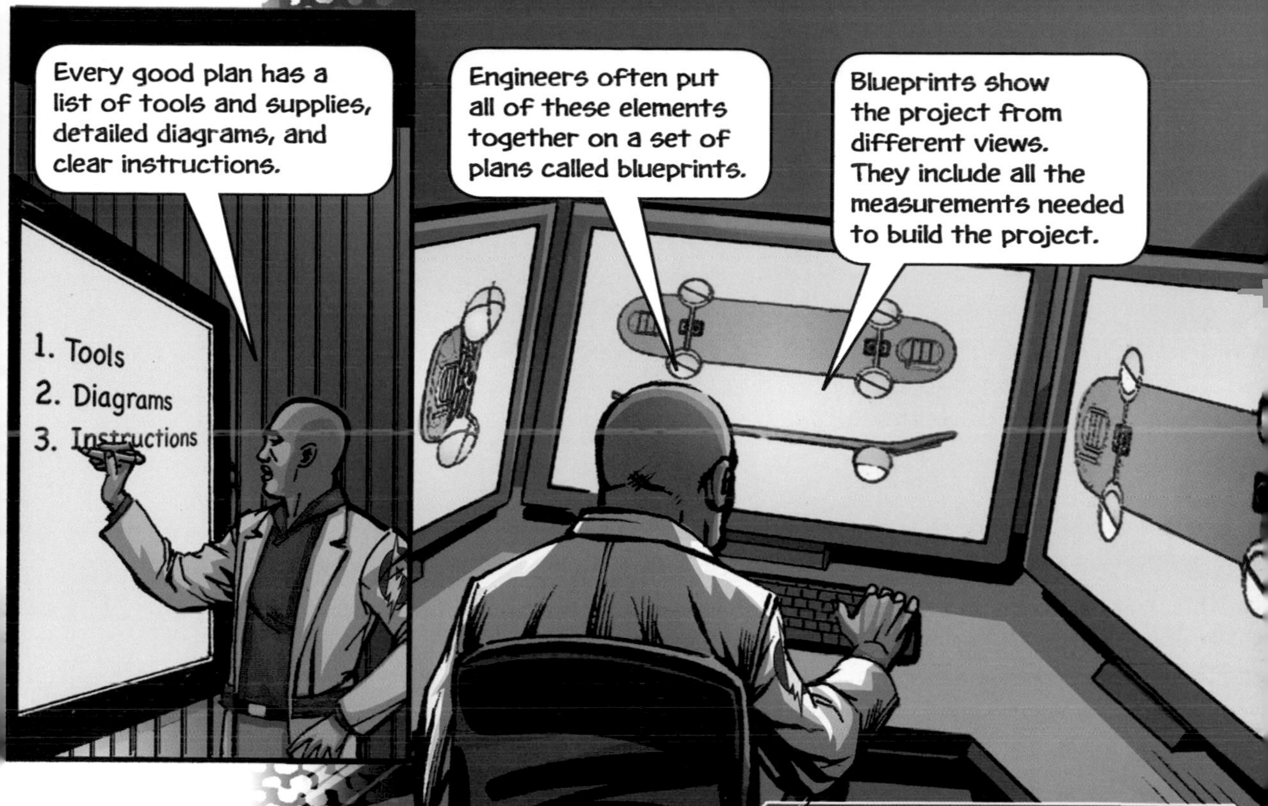
Every good plan has a list of tools and supplies, detailed diagrams, and clear instructions.
1. Tools
2. Diagrams
3. Instructions
Engineers often put all of these elements together on a set of plans called blueprints.
Blueprints show the project from different views. They include all the measurements needed to build the project.

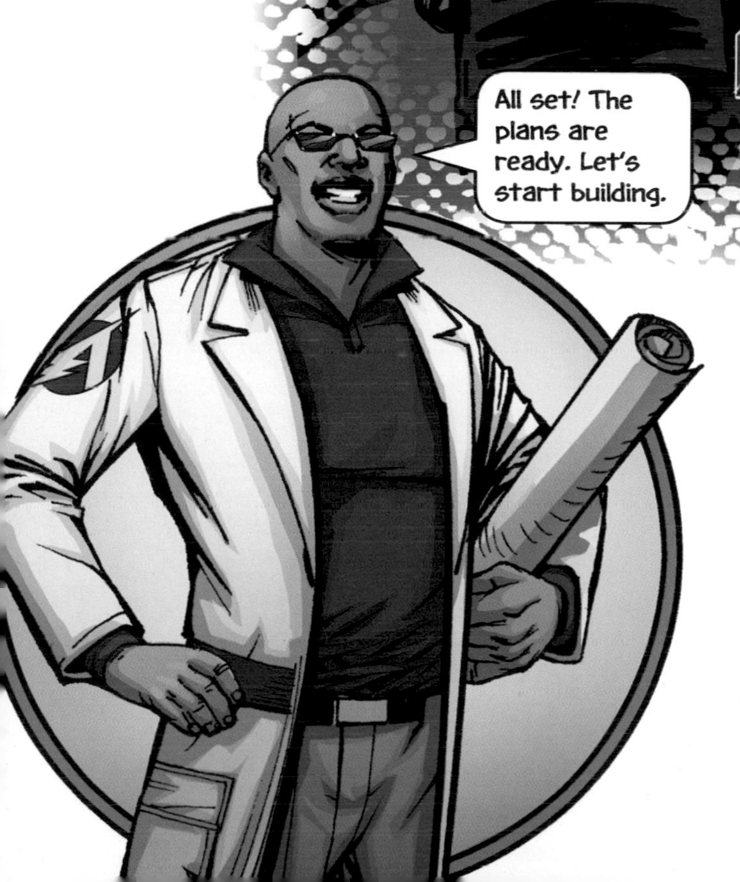
All set! The plans are ready. Let's start building.

BLUEPRINTS

Blueprints are detailed engineering drawings on large sheets of paper. Originally chemical processes were used to copy these large drawings. Older processes produced drawings with blue backgrounds and white lines. Newer processes produce drawings with white backgrounds and blue lines. Today large printers produce black and white drawings, but they are still called blueprints.

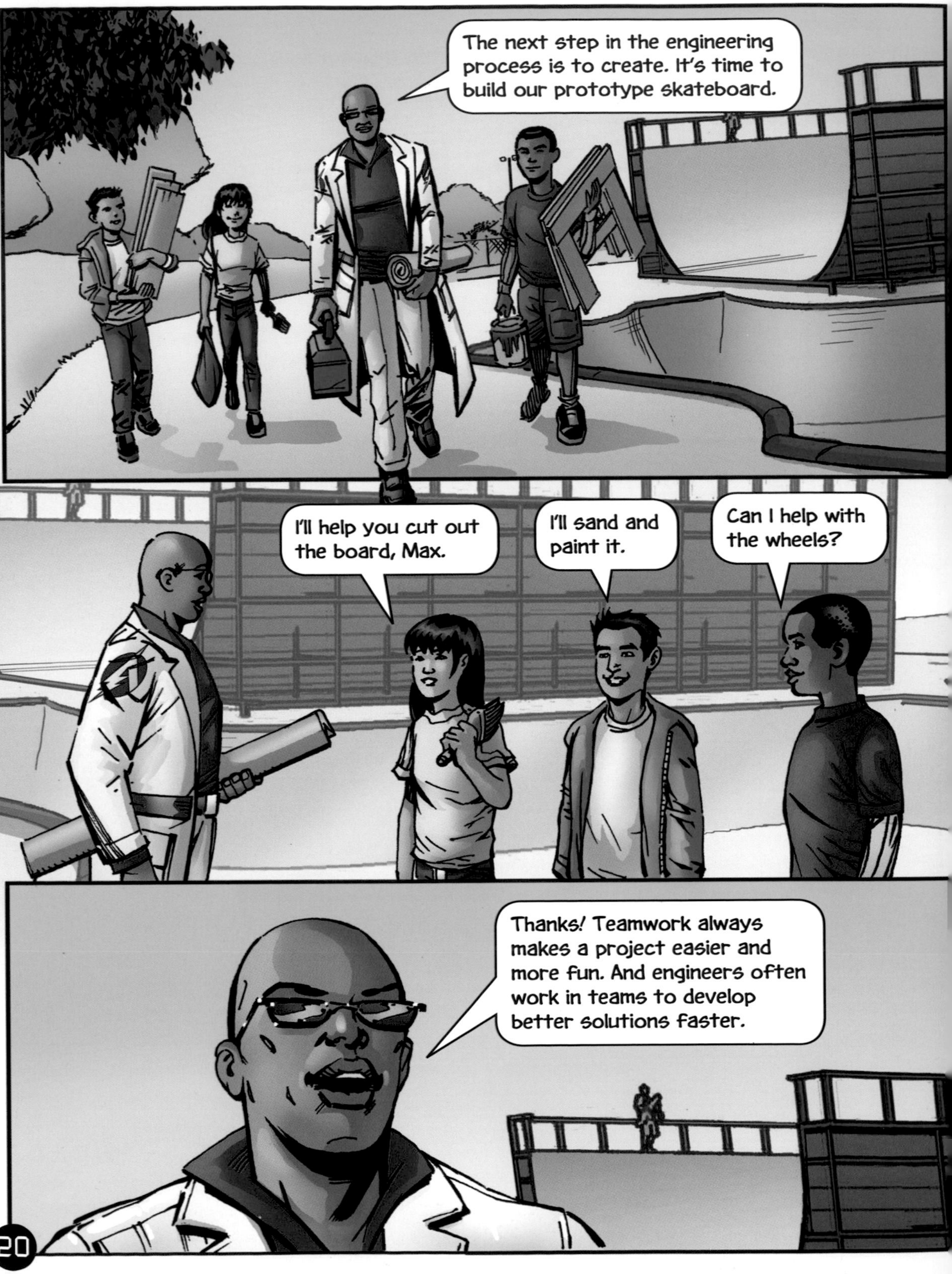
The next step in the engineering process is to create. It's time to build our prototype skateboard.
I'll help you cut out the board, Max.
I'll sand and paint it.
Can I help with the wheels?
Thanks! Teamwork always makes a project easier and more fun. And engineers often work in teams to develop better solutions faster.

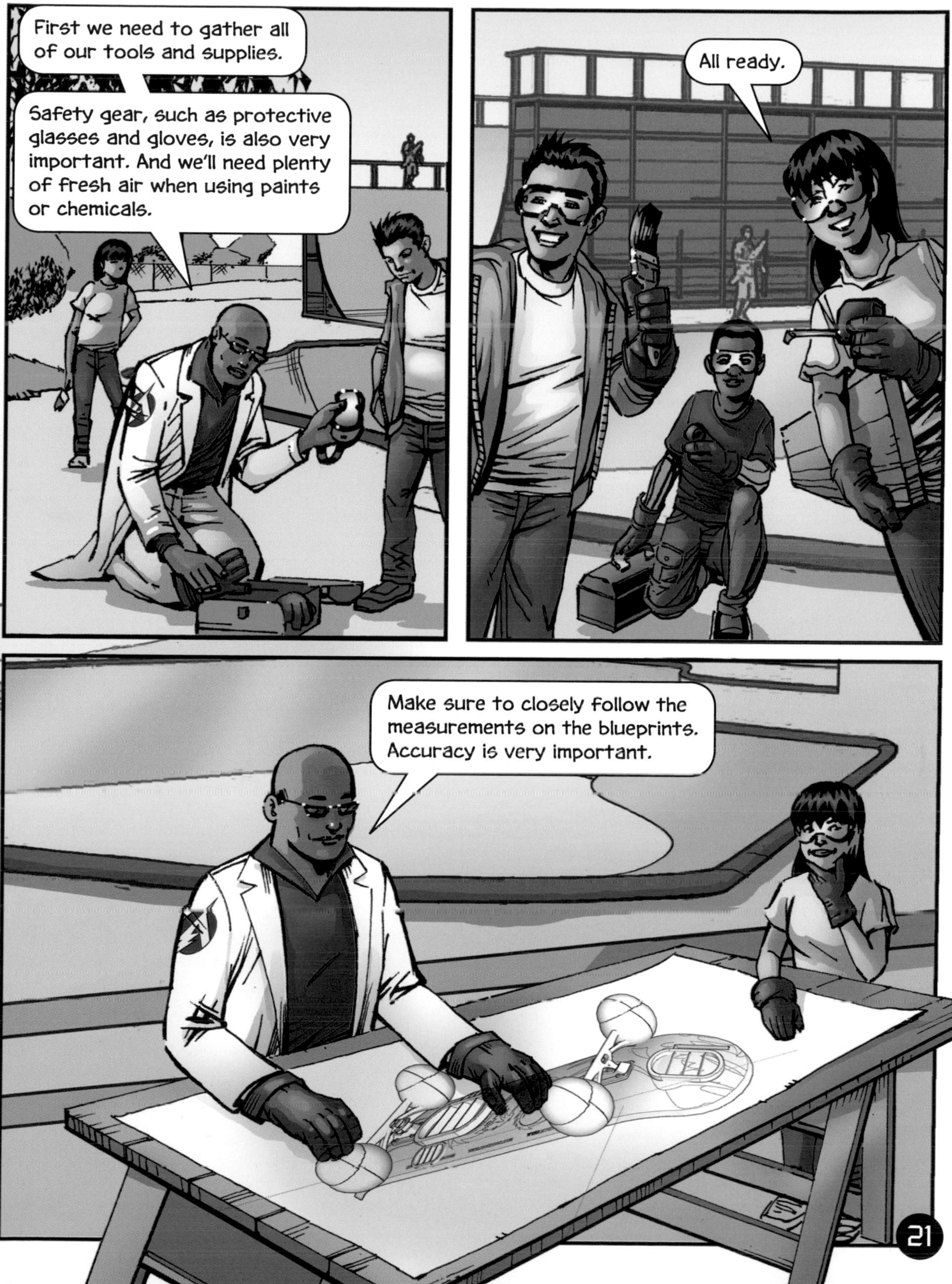
First we need to gather all of our tools and supplies.
Safety gear, such as protective glasses and gloves, is also very important. And we'll need plenty of fresh air when using paints or chemicals.
All ready.
Make sure to closely follow the measurements on the blueprints. Accuracy is very important.

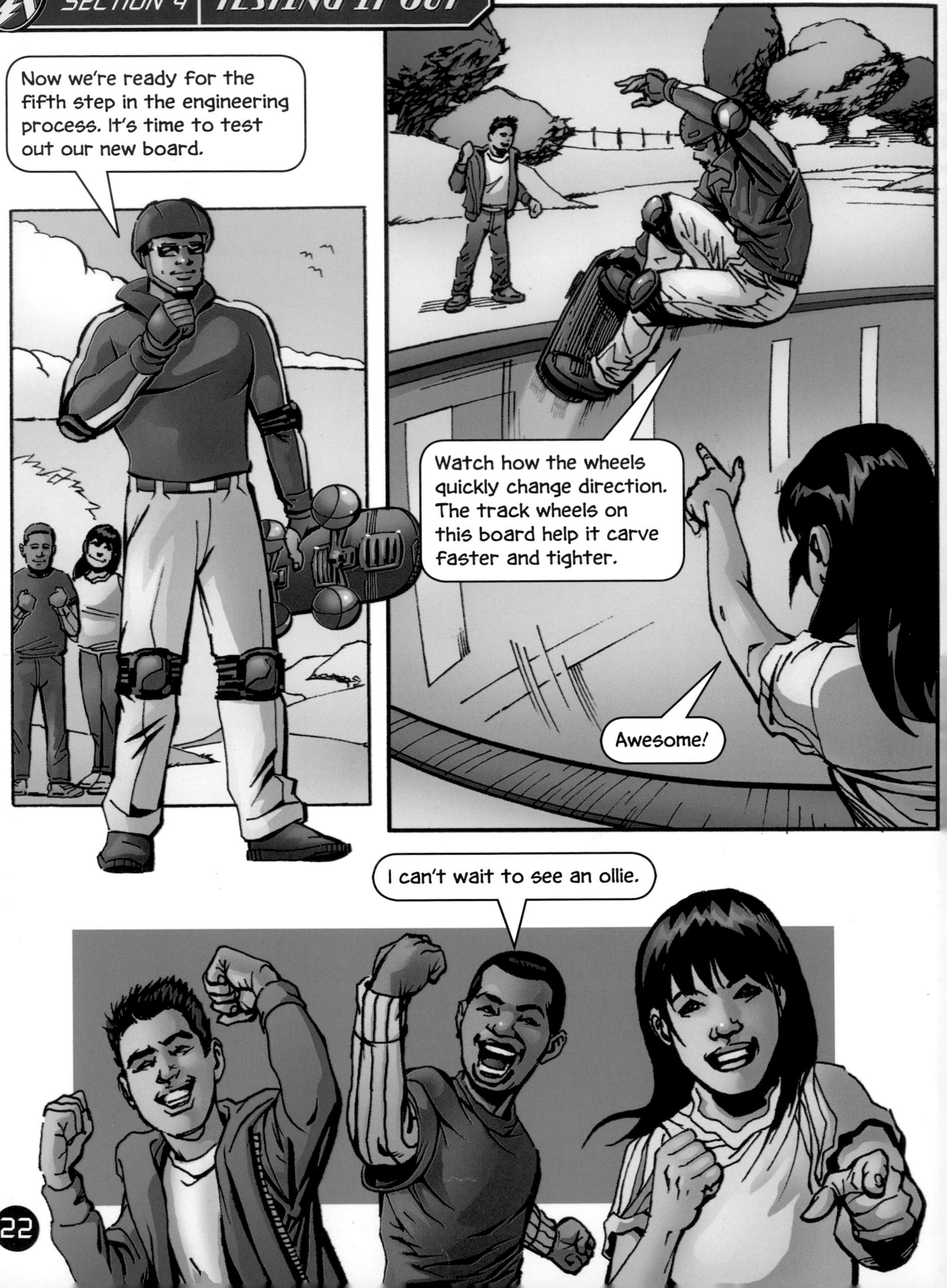
Now we're ready for the fifth step in the engineering process. It's time to test out our new board.
Watch how the wheels quickly change direction. The track wheels on this board help it carve faster and tighter.
Awesome!
I can't wait to see an ollie.

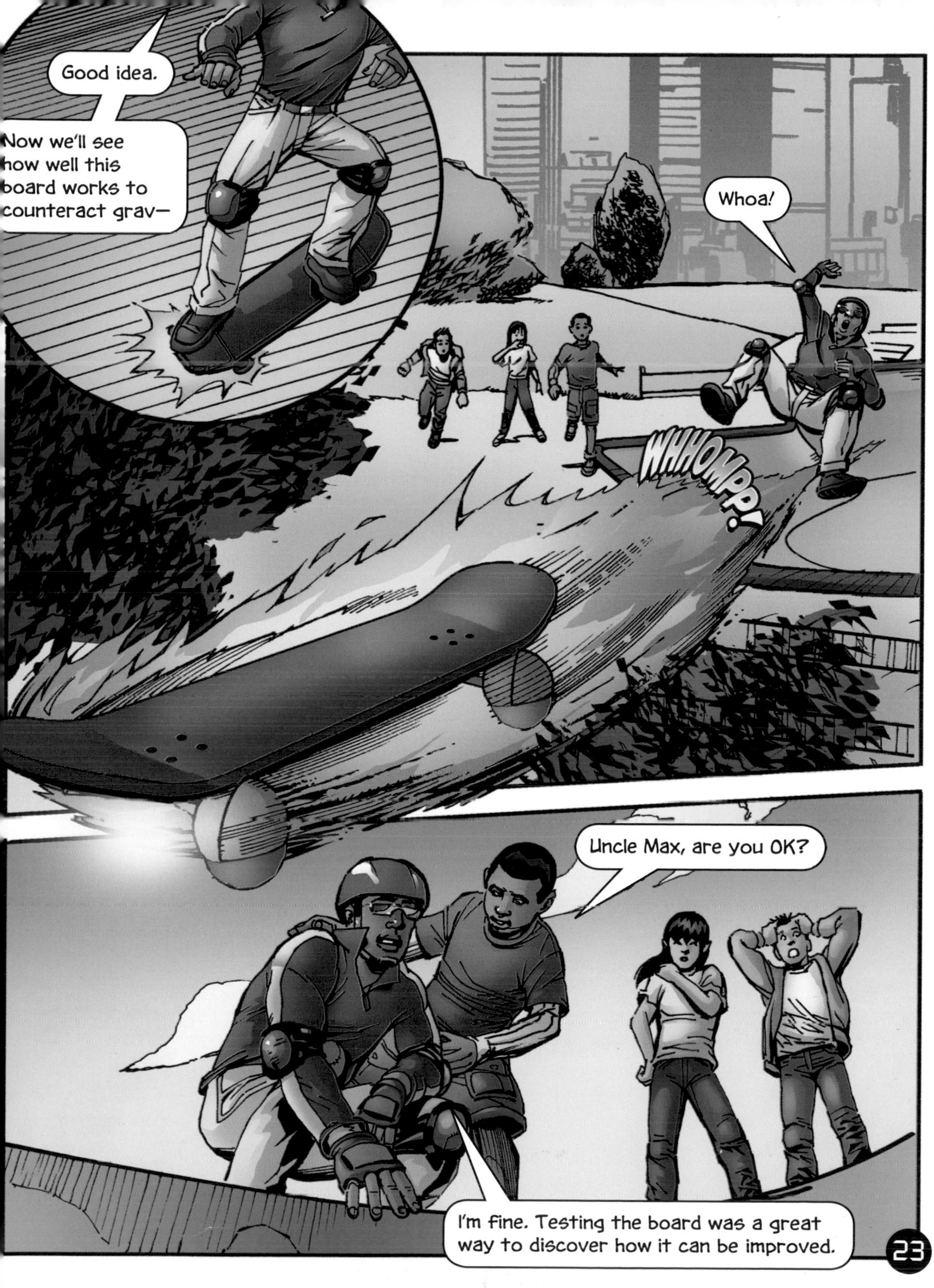
Good idea.
Now we'll see how well this board works to counteract grav—
Whoa!
WHHOMPP!
Uncle Max, are you OK?
I'm fine. Testing the board was a great way to discover how it can be improved.

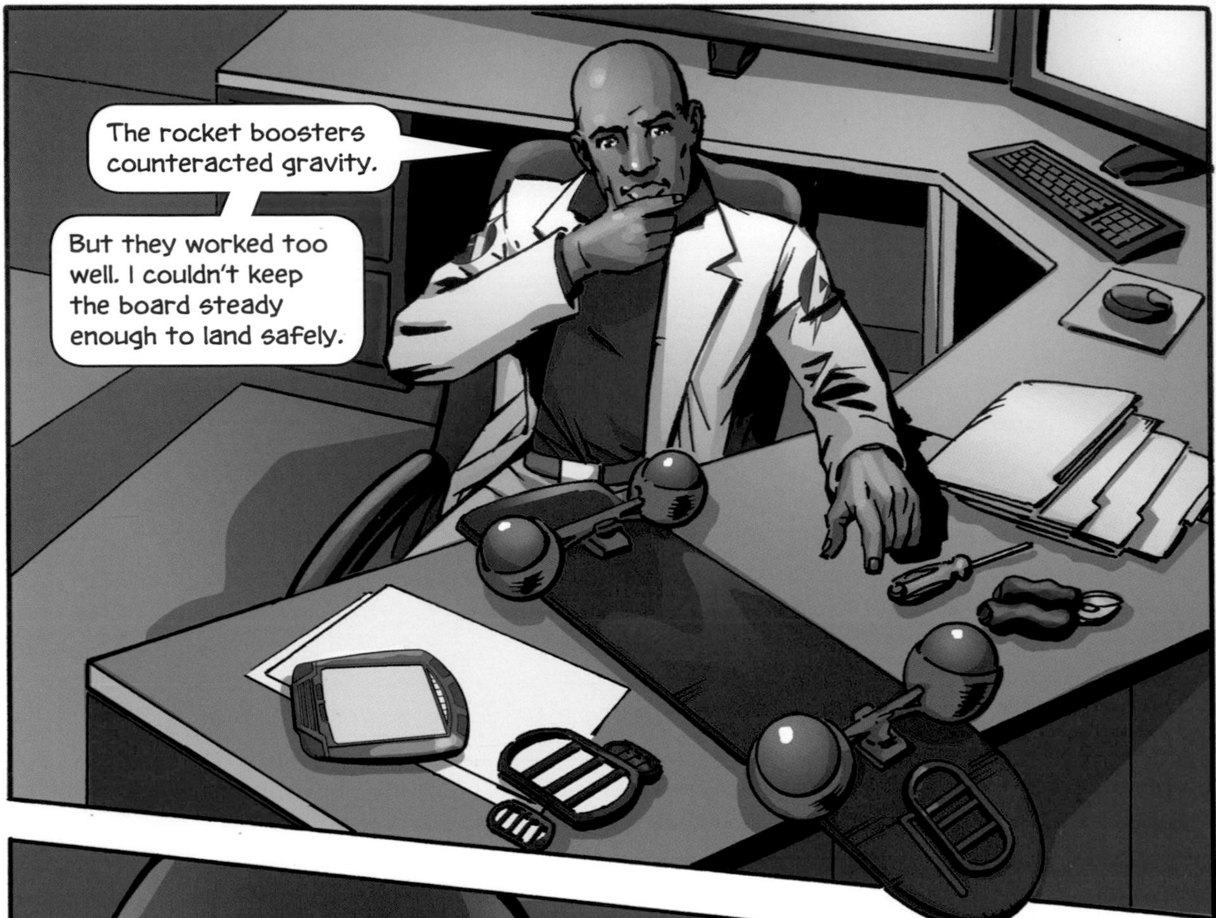
The rocket boosters counteracted gravity.
But they worked too well. I couldn't keep the board steady enough to land safely.

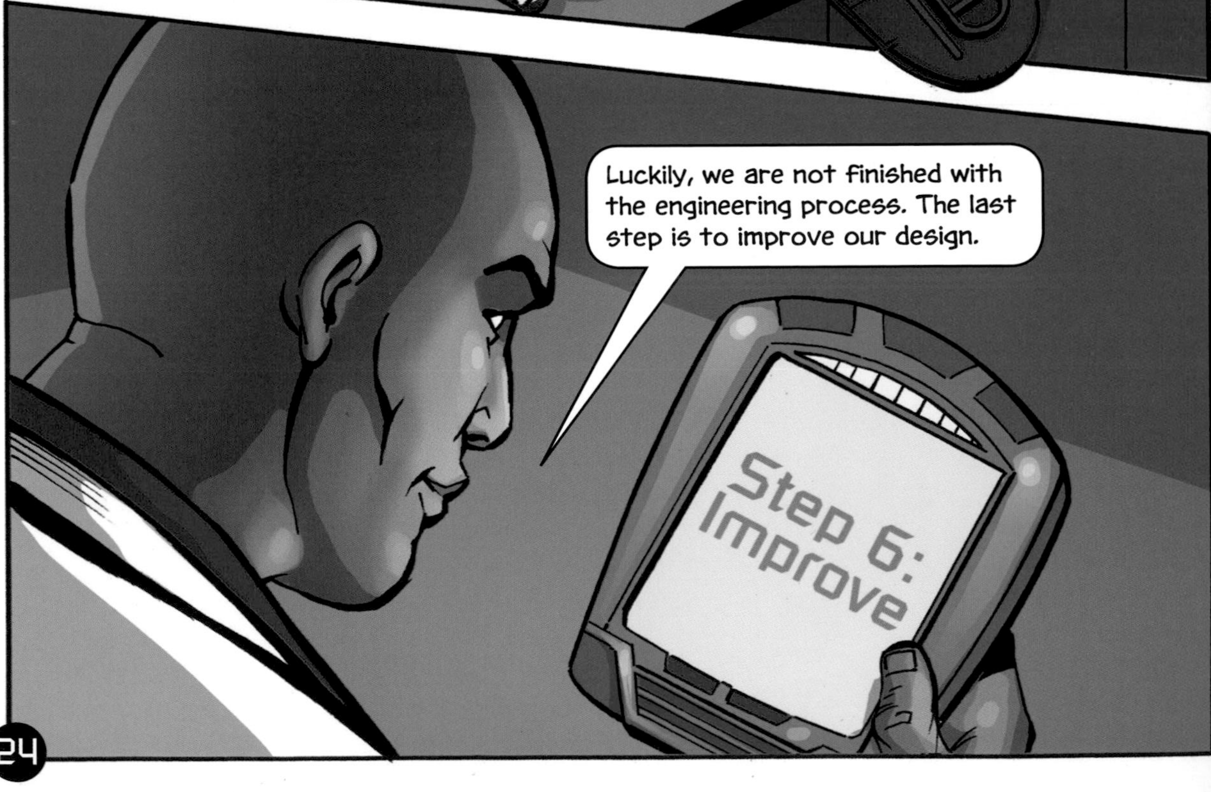
Luckily, we are not finished with the engineering process. The last step is to improve our design.
Step 6: Improve

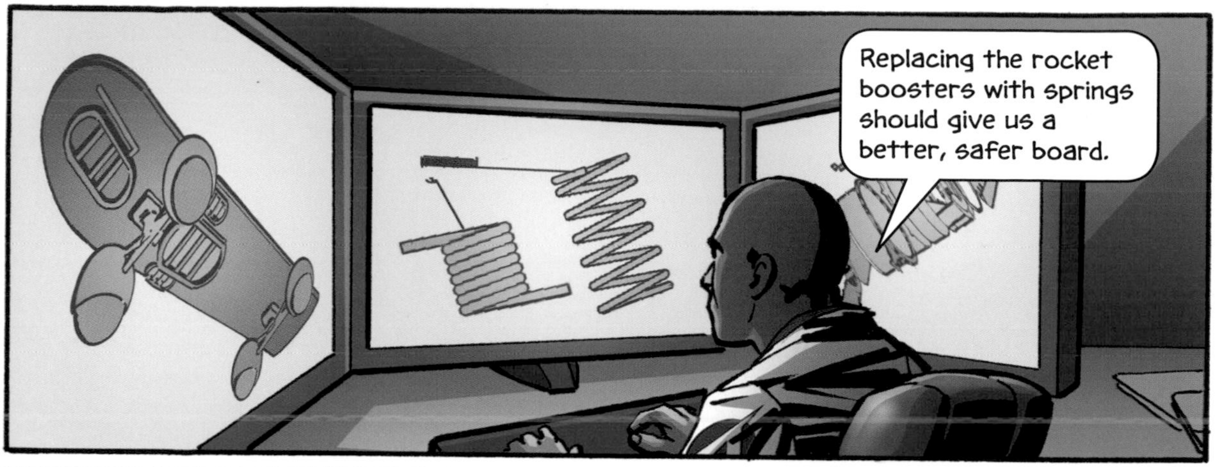
Replacing the rocket boosters with springs should give us a better, safer board.

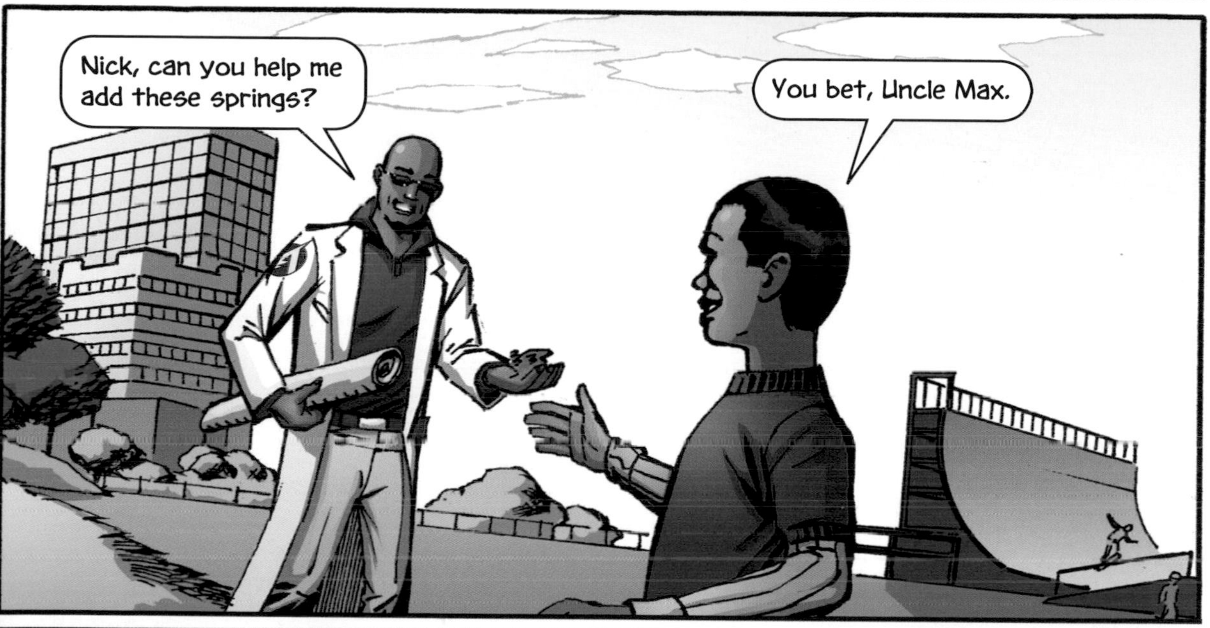
Nick, can you help me add these springs?
You bet, Uncle Max.

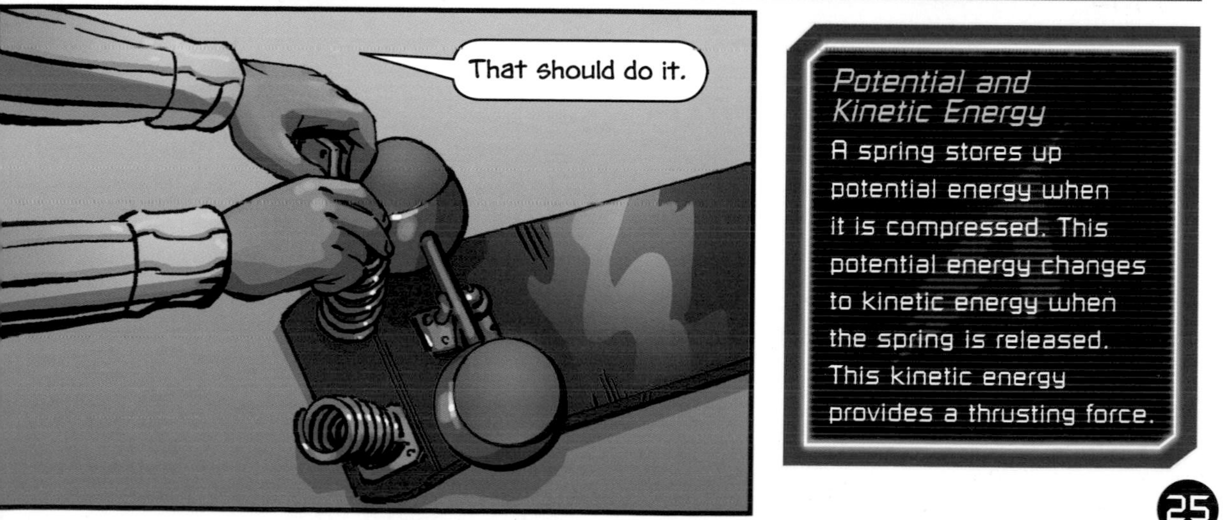
That should do it.

Potential and Kinetic Energy

A spring stores up potential energy when it is compressed. This potential energy changes to kinetic energy when the spring is released. This kinetic energy provides a thrusting force.

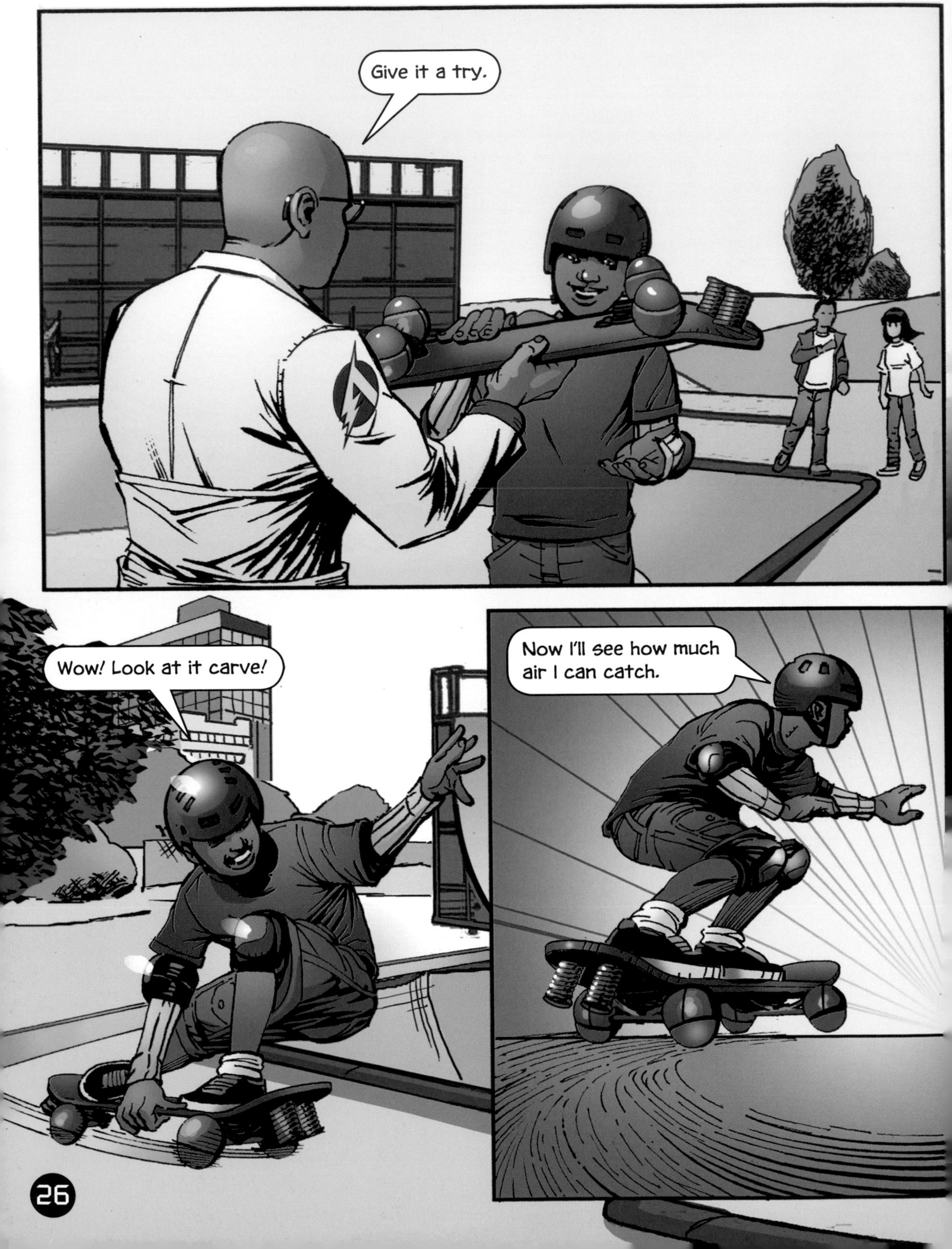
Give it a try.
Wow! Look at it carve!
Now I'll see how much air I can catch.

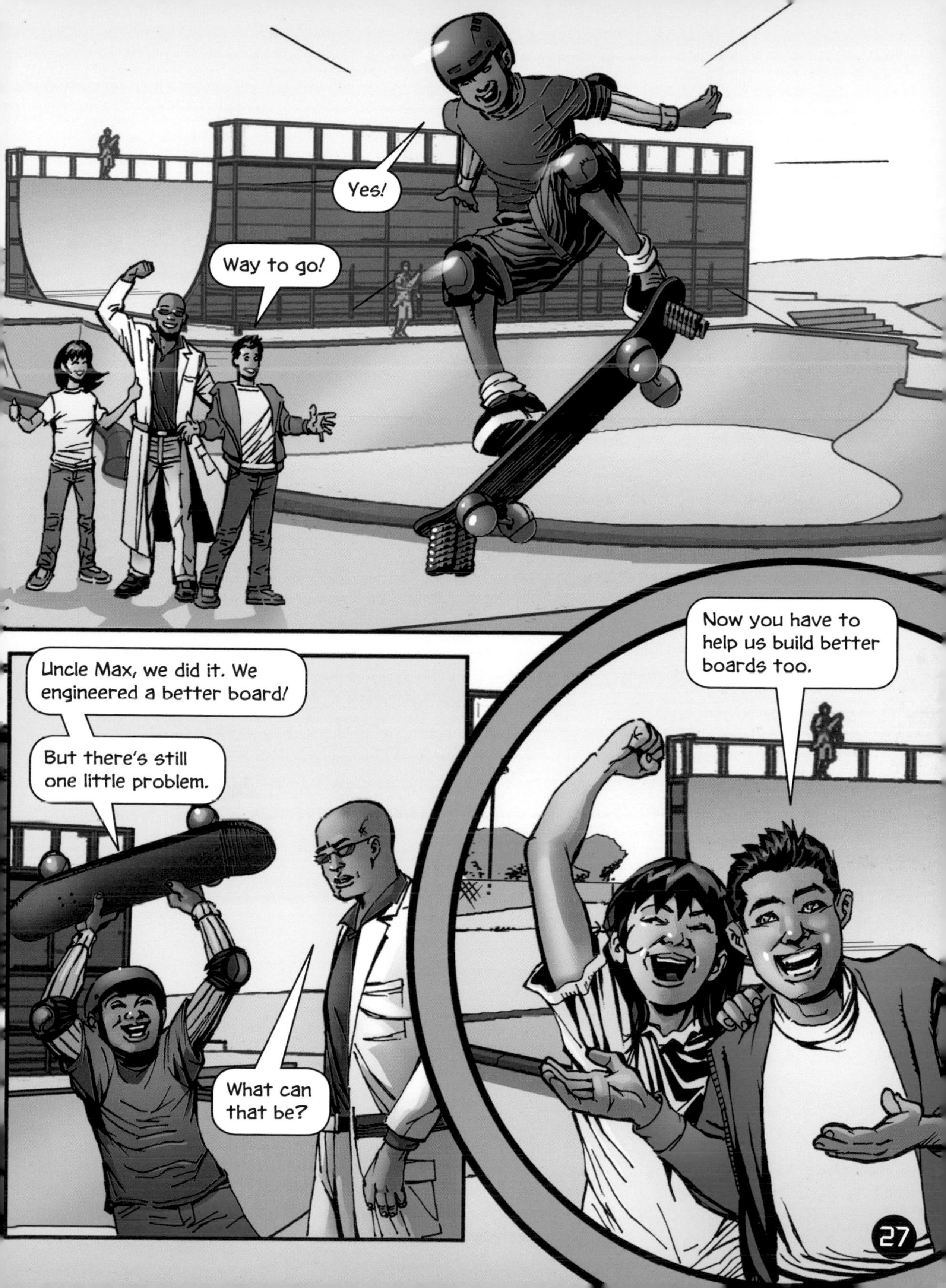

Yes!
Way to go!
Uncle Max, we did it. We engineered a better board!
But there's still one little problem.
What can that be?
Now you have to help us build better boards too.

MORE ABOUT COOL INVENTIONS

- The first skateboards were invented in the 1950s. They were popular with California surfers who became known as "sidewalk surfers." Nobody knows who built the first skateboard, but early boards were nothing like today's models. They were simply wooden boards attached to roller skate wheels.

- The first known roller skates were invented in the 1760s. But these in-line skates, with a single row of wheels, were hard to use. In the 1860s, roller skates with two pairs of wheels were invented. They became the most popular type of roller skate for the next 120 years. In the 1980s, brothers Scott and Brennan Olson rediscovered in-line skates. Through clever engineering, they designed a braking system and buckles that made their in-line skates easy to use. They founded Rollerblade, Inc., and in-line skating quickly became popular.

- Roger Adams never thought of himself as an engineer. But one day he had an idea while watching kids skating near a beach. What if he could make shoes that rolled on command just by shifting one's weight? He started by coming up with ways to combine running shoes and skateboard parts. His skillful engineering paid off big. Now millions of Heelys, shoes with wheels in the heels, have been sold worldwide.

- The Segway is an engineering marvel. It is not quite a bicycle and not quite a car. It has two wheels and stands upright on its own. The rider stands and steers the Segway by simply leaning his or her body. It can travel outside or inside buildings and trains.

Personal jet pack technology has started taking off. Jet packs have been engineered to burn hydrogen peroxide, gasoline, and jet fuel. Flying is the fun part. Engineers are still trying to figure out ways to safely land with a jet pack. One model, the Jetlev Flyer uses water to propel the rider. Since it is used only over water, landings are a lot less dangerous.

Imagine cruising down the road in your car when a sudden burst of speed takes you into the sky. Flying cars aren't as futuristic as you might think. The Terrafugia Transition can travel up to 70 miles (113 kilometers) per hour on the road and 115 miles (185 km) per hour in the air. It switches from driving to flying in less than 30 seconds.

MORE ABOUT

MAX AXIOM

SUPER SCIENTIST

Real name: Maxwell J. Axiom
Hometown: Seattle, Washington
Height: 6' 1"   Weight: 192 lbs
Eyes: Brown   Hair: None

Super capabilities: Super intelligence; able to shrink to the size of an atom; sunglasses give x-ray vision; lab coat allows for travel through time and space.

Origin: Since birth, Max Axiom seemed destined for greatness. His mother, a marine biologist, taught her son about the mysteries of the sea. His father, a nuclear physicist and volunteer park ranger, schooled Max on the wonders of earth and sky.

One day on a wilderness hike, a megacharged lightning bolt struck Max with blinding fury. When he awoke, Max discovered a newfound energy and set out to learn as much about science as possible. He traveled the globe earning degrees in every aspect of the field. Upon his return, he was ready to share his knowledge and new identity with the world. He had become Max Axiom, Super Scientist.

GLOSSARY

angular momentum (ANG-gyu-lur moh-MEN-tuhm)—a physics concept related to how something rotates around a point

blueprint (BLOO-print)—diagram that shows how to construct a building or other project

carve (KAHRV)—to make sharp turns on a skateboard without skidding

counteract (koun-tur-AKT)—to act against something so that it is less effective

gravity (GRAV-uh-tee)—a force that pulls objects with mass together; gravity pulls objects down toward the center of Earth

hydrogen peroxide (HYE-druh-juhn puh-ROCKS-eyed)—a colorless liquid often used to kill germs

kinetic energy (ki-NET-ik EN-ur-jee)—the energy of a moving object

physics (FIZ-iks)—the science that deals with matter and energy; physics includes the study of light, heat, sound, electricity, motion, and force

potential energy (puh-TEN-shuhl EN-ur-jee)—the stored energy of an object that is raised, stretched, or squeezed

prototype (PROH-tuh-tipe)—the first version of an invention that tests an idea to see if it will work

rotate (ROH-tate)—to spin around

thrust (THRUHST)—the force that pushes an object forward

READ MORE

Brasch, Nicolas. *Triumphs of Engineering.* Discovery Education: Technology. New York: PowerKids Press, 2013.

Enz, Tammy. *Build It: Invent New Structures and Contraptions.* Invent It. North Mankato, Minn.: Capstone Press, 2012.

Gonzales, Doreen. *What Are the 7 Wonders of the Modern World?* Berkeley Heights, N.J.: Enslow Publishers, 2012.

Herweck, Don. *Mechanical Engineering.* Mission, Science. Mankato, Minn.: Compass Point Books, 2009.

Way, Steve, and Gerry Bailey. *Structures.* Simply Science. Pleasantville, N.Y.: Gareth Stevens Pub., 2009.

INTERNET SITES

FactHound offers a safe, fun way to find Internet sites related to this book. All sites on FactHound have been researched by our staff.

Here's all you do:

Visit *www.facthound.com*

Type in this code: 9781429699358

Super-cool stuff! Check out projects, games and lots more at
www.capstonekids.com

INDEX